managing your memory

managing your memory

A concise
and straightforward guide to
making your memory work for you!

Harold L. Taylor

HAROLD TAYLOR
TIME CONSULTANTS INC.
2175 Sheppard Ave. E., Suite 110, Willowdale, Ontario M2J 1W8

Artwork by Ruth Lemkay

First Edition
Published in the United States by Beaufort Books, Inc.
Published in Canada by General Publishing Co. Limited

Second Edition
Published by Harold Taylor Time Consultants Inc.

Canadian Cataloguing in Publication Data

Taylor, Harold, 1934-
Managing your memory

Bibliography: p.
ISBN 0-9691407-5-4

1. Mnemonics – Popular works. I. Title.
BF371.T39 1988 153.1'2 C88-094805-1

Printed in Canada

TABLE OF CONTENTS

Dedication:

To Marlene, my back-up memory system

INTRODUCTION

This morning, 75,485 housewives couldn't remember whether they had put sugar in their coffee, and had to taste it to find out. 16,580 business executives left their briefcases in the front hallway when they went to work. 97,280 school children forgot their lunches on the kitchen table.

The above figures are fictitious. The situations are not. Poor memory is costing society billions of dollars annually. Umbrellas are left in restaurants. Doors are left unlocked and houses are being ransacked. Sales are being lost. Products on assembly lines are being rejected. People are becoming inconvenienced, embarrassed, and humiliated. Machines in plants are left running unguarded. Accidents are occurring. Lives are being lost.

Poor memory can bring ridicule, chaos, or disaster.

And it's all so unnecessary. For people in general don't have poor memories. They simply fail to utilize the memory capacity they were born with. They fail to ***manage*** their memories.

Do you ever forget to take your suit to the cleaners? Are you ever embarrassed because you can't recall a customer's name? Are you ever inconvenienced because you can't remember where you put the spare set of car keys? Of course you are. We ***all*** are on occasion. But these occasions can be reduced to a bare minimum by spending only an hour or two each week training your memory. And only for a few months. For by then, you will be practicing everything you have learned. Managing your memory will become a way of life. It will become automatic.

You will have no trouble reciting the names of a dozen or more people you had met only briefly a few days before. Or remembering a list of twenty items you want to pick up at the store. Or dialing phone numbers of friends and acquaintances without having to look them up in the directory. Or retrieving your spare pair of eyeglasses you had stashed away two years ago.

Follow along with me as I take you through the stages of developing your memory. Don't just ***read*** this book. Practice it. Work along with me and I'll show you how I have improved my own memory. For I'm no memory expert. I was probably worse than you are right now. I picked up, read, and absorbed every book and article I could find on memory training. The books are listed in the bibliography at the back of this book. Some of the techniques seem mind boggling. But we're not studying to be memory experts. We don't have the time, patience, or inclination to commit one hundred "keys" to memory. Nor do we have the need or desire to memorize the Manhattan telephone directory, or the populations of the fifty largest cities, or a hundred meaningless four-digit numbers.

At least ***I*** don't. I'm a manager. And I can't afford the time to become a memory expert. All I need is a good memory. Nothing less. Nothing more. If your needs are greater, get a copy of all those books listed in the bibliography, lock yourself in your room for a few years, and go to it.

But if your goal is less ambitious. If you simply need to be able to manage your memory quickly. With a minimum of effort. With the result that you can remember names and faces, numbers, facts and figures, develop your powers of observation and listening, be able to remember what you read, and overcome absentmindedness, then this book is all you need. Read on.

Chapter 1

How Memory Works

The Long And The Short Of It

Evidence indicates that we possess two separate memory systems: short-term memory and long-term memory. Assuming we pay attention and see or hear the information properly, it is immediately sent into short-term storage. Thus we have no trouble dialing a telephone number immediately upon looking it up or repeating a person's name right after being introduced. But unless we made a conscious effort to memorize the information – to transfer it to long-term storage – the memory of it soon disappears. When this happens you have to look up the telephone number again after getting a busy signal, or ask your spouse the name of the person you both had been introduced to only moments before.

There's a documented case of a man who didn't have any long-term memory system – as a result of an operation to relieve epilepsy. He remembered everything that happened ***before*** his operation, but everything that happened to him ***since*** disappears from his memory almost immediately. His mind has been a blank since 1953. He could read the same magazine every day and the material would seem new to him. He could laugh repeatedly at the same jokes, and be introduced to the same people. A tragic case.

It would also be a tragedy – although a lesser one – if we failed to utilize the abilities we ***do*** have. Including the ability to transfer information to long-term storage.

Assuming we are able to get the information into long-term storage, we still may have a problem recalling the information at a later date. Just how much of a problem we have depends on how effectively we memorized the information.

Quite simply, then, a poor memory is a result of a failure on our part to:

(a) observe or listen closely in order to get the information immediately into our ***short-term*** memory system
(b) consciously attempt to transfer the information into our ***long-term*** storage system
(c) ***provide clues*** for our mind to ***recall*** the information later.

Although they may not say it, or even realize it, every gimmick used by memory experts works only because it forces us to perform one or more of these three activities.

So there's no one best technique. No magical method. There are hundreds of ways you can accomplish the above. And they all require effort on your part. I will show you the methods I use, the ones that require the least effort and seem to work the best.

The rest is up to you.

Chapter 2

The Power Of Observation

Our Miraculous Brain

We have some magnificent God-given senses, controlled by an even more miraculous brain. A brain, whose over ten billion cells perform functions which would be inconceivable for the most sophisticated electronic computer. Those amazing senses such as sight, hearing, touch, smell, are wasted on most of us. We barely use them. Our eyes are open but we don't really observe.

I used to walk the eight or ten blocks to my office. After several weeks someone asked me where the closest service station was located. I was baffled. I remembered passing one, but not only could I not give its exact location, I didn't know what brand of gas they sold. Or whether it was a self-serve or regular station. Nor could I describe many of the other stores along the route.

And when I was asked directions to my ***own house,*** I couldn't relate street names other than the few on either side of our house. I used to tell visitors "our street is about the third or fourth one on the left-hand side." And yet I had walked or jogged or driven that route for over a year! Disgraceful. It would have taken no more effort to check the signs and become familiar with my surroundings as I took my daily walk. And yet so many of us are like that. We don't truly observe. No wonder we miss half the beauty in the world.

When I became interested in memory training, and realized that I would have to change my habits and start observing and listening, what a transformation. I saw beautiful gardens I had never seen before, birds I didn't know existed, interesting people, strange buildings. I laughed at the terrible colors on some people's houses, marvelled at the cleanliness of yards, was appalled by the junk stored in garages. I ***saw*** for the first time. I could describe every building, tell which restaurants were open at 7:30 a.m., identify the people who waited at the same bus stop. I knew the names of the streets, could tell which ones were one-way streets, which ones had boulevards.

No special techniques. No memory gimmicks. Simply the ***desire*** to start observing. To utilize the precious asset called sight. How tragic that some people don't have sight. And most of us who do have it, waste it by not using it fully.

We cannot expect to remember a face which we didn't really see. Or recall a street name we didn't read. Or find a book we carelessly stashed somewhere without thinking. If you are really sincere about improving your memory, you will have to consciously ***observe.***

Unless you are observant, your attempts at managing your memory will fail. Repetition is not enough.

Do you know which side the Queen's head is facing on a Canadian dime? Most people in my seminars tell me it's to the left. Which is wrong. And yet they've seen thousands of dimes. Most of them could not tell me whose picture was on the five-dollar bill – or ***any*** of the bills for that matter. Or whether their wristwatch bore a roman numeral "VI" or an arabic "6". Or which letters were opposite the number 7 on a telephone dial. You probably can't either, because you have had no real desire to ***observe*** these things. Who ***cares*** what the name of the person next door is? Who cares what the name of the street next to ours is? Who cares what the boss's telephone number is? Nobody cares! That is until they want to ***remember*** those things. But by then, it's too late.

We cannot remember what we don't truly observe. We leave our remembering until too late. Our habit of not really ***observing*** is trapping us into letting even important things slip by us.

Make up your mind ***now*** that you are going to truly ***observe*** everything that comes within your range of sight. It takes no more time. No more effort. Since you're already looking at it, you might as well ***observe*** it.

You must truly ***observe*** something before it can be registered into your short-term memory. So open your eyes wide. Practice studying the features of fellow passengers in the bus or subway. Practice taking in your surroundings when you go for a walk or attend a meeting. You will soon acquire the ***power of observation.***

The first step in managing your memory.

Chapter 3

Listen! Listen! Listen!

'Hear' Is The Way To Do It!

Most of us are poor listeners. And listening, like observation, is essential to good memory. We normally forget twenty-five percent of everything we hear within two months of hearing it. To not hear it correctly in the first place would be disastrous.

Be an active listener as well as an active observer. You cannot remember anything you never really hear in the first place. It just won't make it into your short-term memory. When you meet someone for the first time, pay attention. Listen carefully for the name. Ask him or her to repeat it if you don't hear it properly. Repeat the name as soon as possible after the introduction and use it throughout the conversation. Your short-term memory is a temporary storage device which accepts indiscriminately any information which has commanded your attention. So get in the habit of being an active listener and observer. Information you're not really interested in retaining will soon disappear from temporary storage. But in the meantime, capture it while you have the chance.

It's easier to capture faces than names since visual images register on our brains with little effort on our part. Consequently, people seldom have trouble remembering faces – only the names that go with them. You don't hear many people complaining "your name is familiar but I can't recall your face."

Be genuinely interested in people. Long-term memories are created out of short-term memories which remain active long enough. To keep the memory of names active, use them frequently, repeat them to yourself, write them down when you get a chance. Show an interest in the owners of the names – their looks, personalities, jobs, hobbies, backgrounds. If we concentrate on information, whether it be names, faces, facts or numbers – mull it over, repeat it, visualize it. It will move into long-term storage.

New memories are vulnerable to disruption before they are fully set into long-term storage. So don't allow yourself to be distracted when meeting people for the first time. Give them your undivided attention. Spend a few minutes talking to them and mulling over their names while observing their features. Don't be pushed into meeting a dozen people in rapid succession.

Studies also indicate that while under the influence of alcohol our short-term memories are not affected. But we lose our ability to transfer information into long-term memory. So don't be surprised if you can't recall the names of people you met at a party last night.

You're probably interested in remembering more than just names. You will want to recall the points made by a speaker, the decisions reached at a meeting, the suggestions made by an employee or friend. And the longer a person talks, the more difficult it is to listen.

We can speak at about one hundred and twenty-five words per minute, but we can listen about four times as fast. With all this spare time to kill, our mind wanders, daydreams, takes little mental excursions and frequently doesn't get back to the speaker in time. We miss points, meanings. We guess. Misinterpret. We can't slow down our thinking process, but we can utilize the spare time more effectively. The secret is to ***stay with the speaker.*** Review and mentally summarize what he has said. Listen between the lines, look for those non-verbal gestures. Weigh the evidence being used to support his points. But ***stick with him.*** Don't drift into space or start formulating your own reply while he's still speaking. Effective listening pays big dividends and courses in improving listening skills would go a long way in improving your memory.

But they're not necessary. Not if you have really made up your mind that you are going to improve your memory. By observing. By listening. And by following the exercises in this book.

Memory improvement is no different than any other area of self-development. You succeed when the desire to succeed becomes great enough.

Chapter 4

Give Your Mind A Clue

The Power of Recall

If you make a conscious effort to remember names, faces or information, it will move into a permanent filing system called long-term memory. However, there is sometimes a problem in retrieving the information when you need it. This can be overcome by providing clues so your mind can recall it later. You do this when you learn as much as possible about people when you meet them. The more you know about a person, the more associations you can make and the more clues you will have in your mind to remind you of his or her name later.

So if you want to recall the name of a man you met last week, concentrate on everything you learned about him, everything that happened on the occasion you met him; appearance, personality, events connected with him. Eventually one of these events or characteristics will stimulate recall of his name from long-term memory. For recall from permanent memory involves a process of association whereby one memory evokes another. This is evident when you hear a familiar song which evokes memories of events that were associated with it, or you pass a familiar landmark that reminds you of something that happened there in the past.

Think back to your early school days. What clues did the teacher suggest in order to make it easier for you to recall information? Some of the memory aids or "gimmicks" are probably still with you today. For instance, what is R.O.Y. G. B.I.V.? For me, it was the colors of the rainbow: red, orange, yellow, green, blue, indigo and violet. It still is. For once information has been transferred to long-term memory, it stays there until recalled. And the fictional name, R.O.Y. G. B.I.V. is enough of a clue to enable it to be recalled.

Do you know the names of the great lakes bordering Canada and the U.S.A.? Easy, they're H.O.M.E.S.

Which translated means Huron, Ontario, Michigan, Erie and Superior. A flimsy clue when you think about it. For the letter "H" could stand for thousands of names. But once we have learned that the name of the lake is Huron, all we need is the first letter "H" to remind us of it. To recall it from long-term storage we ***associate*** the letter "H" with the full name, Huron.

What other recall clues have you learned? How about "spring forward and fall back" when changing from standard time to daylight saving time? Or the little rhyme, "30 days has September, April, June and November..." or "Every Good Boy Deserves Favor" as the lines of the treble clef of the musical staff.

If you associated clues such as these to remember information ten or twenty years ago, chances are you will still be able to recall the information today. For the brain is an amazing thing. It remembers everything you put there. All you need is a way of extracting it at will.

One last clue. What does A.I.R. stand for? Well, it's ***Attention, Interest*** and ***Repetition.*** That's how you get information into long-term storage in the first place. That's what we were talking about in the last chapter. Don't forget it. I'm leaving it up to you now to give names, faces or facts your undivided ***attention.*** To be ***interested*** in remembering them. And to ***repeat*** them to yourself – even write them down if possible. Remember to ***observe.*** And ***listen.*** This will insure that they get into your brain's long-term storage system.

In the following chapters I'll show you how you can get them ***out.***

Chapter 5

Organized Thinking

Memory Links

It's a proven fact that we remember things we ***understand*** a lot better than those things we commit to memory by rote without really grasping their ***meaning.*** It takes ten times as long to commit meaningless words to memory than those that make sense.

As an example, take a look at the following lists of words. Which list do you think you can remember the easiest?

List 1	*List 2*	*List 3*
Goy	Truck	Why
Win	Tag	Do
Gul	Mine	You
Bof	Horse	Want
Seb	Bag	To
Zim	Pail	Improve
Yog	Dog	Your
Tob	Trail	Power
Jik	Tree	Of
Aig	Gown	Recall

It's difficult to remember list 1. The words don't make sense. List 2 is easier. At least they are words that we can ***visualize.*** List 3 is a snap. The words not only make sense, they are organized in such a way that recalling one word tells you what the next word will be. You can remember ***and*** recall list 3 in a matter of seconds.

To recall information easier, always put as much meaning as possible into it. Organize it in such a way that it will be easy to recall. And ***visualize*** it.

Here's an example of how you can memorize the twenty-five largest cities in North America, ***in order,*** in less than fifteen minutes. It takes longer to ***describe*** the process than to ***do*** it. So bear with me.

According to my information, here are the twenty-five largest cities in descending order of population:

1. New York
2. Los Angeles
3. Chicago
4. Philadelphia
5. Detroit
6. San Francisco
7. Washington
8. Montreal
9. Toronto
10. Boston
11. Pittsburgh
12. St. Louis
13. Baltimore
14. Cleveland
15. Houston
16. Newark
17. Minneapolis
18. Dallas
19. Anaheim
20. Seattle
21. Milwaukee
22. Cincinnati
23. Atlanta
24. Patterson, N.J.
25. Buffalo

Okay. What we want to do first, is ***visualize*** New York. Then we want to remember it in such a way that recalling New York will help us recall the next one, "Los Angeles" and so on.

Pick something as a clue or symbol for New York. Let's say the Statue of Liberty. Now ***picture*** the Statue of Liberty, arm upraised holding the torch. Circling around that torch, visualize a bunch of ***angels.*** See them in your mind's eye. Put action into it. They are flapping their wings furiously.

Now when you think of the largest city you will see the Statue of Liberty, which represents New York. But that's not all. You will also see angels circling the outstretched arm, which will remind you of ***Los Angeles.*** Angel does not have to sound exactly the same as Los Angeles. It's close enough to provide the clue that will allow you to recall ***Los Angeles.***

Now you simply continue building a story as you go. Visualize symbols or clues to represent the cities and link them in some way to the previous city. So the ***angels*** are reaching up with both hands and grabbing hold of the legs of some giant yellow ***chicks*** flying overhead. The fact that chickens don't fly is immaterial. The more ridiculous your picture, the better.

Make it wild, colorful, with lots of action. And you won't be able to forget it. The ***chicks'*** heads are covered with ***Philadelphia*** cream cheese. It's oozing over their eyes, beaks and necks.

And there is a ***car*** symbolic of ***Detroit*** spinning wheels in this cream cheese. It's stuck. Cheese is flying all over the place as it tries to get free.

Now pause for a minute. Here's how your recall should work. What's the largest city in North America? Why ***New York,*** of course. And immediately you picture the Statue of Liberty with it's arm outstretched. What is flying around that arm? ***Angels.*** Which reminds you of ***Los Angeles.*** What's happening with the angels? They're grabbing hold of some ***chicks*** flying overhead. ***Chicago.*** What's happening with the chicks? They've got ***Philadelphia*** cream cheese all over their heads. ***Philadelphia.*** What's happening with the cheese? There's a car stuck in it, spinning its wheels. ***Detroit.***

Already we've got the five largest cities memorized in order. Let's continue. What's happening with the car that's stuck? It has this huge cable attached to it with a ***cable car*** running along it. ***San Francisco.***

And hanging from the cable is all kinds of ***washing. Washington.***

And a ***French-Canadian*** is painting fleur de lys and Canadian flags all over the laundry. ***Montreal.***

And suddenly, a huge needle-like structure is stuck right through all those painted flags – it's the ***C.N. Tower,*** symbolic of ***Toronto.***

As you visualize the C.N. Tower, you see a giant pot dumping ***Boston*** baked beans all over it. ***Boston.***

I'm making the pictures brief now. But don't *you* do it. Make every picture vivid, imaginative and lively. See those huge brown beans and sauce dripping down the C.N. Tower, covering the windows on the observation deck, and dropping in gobs to the pavement below. It only takes seconds to visualize a descriptive scene in your mind's eye. So make it a vision that will not easily fade from your memory.

So far you've committed ten cities, in order, to memory. Review them quickly:

1. ***Statue of Liberty*** with arm outstretched = New York

2. ***Angels*** circling around the outstretched arm = Los Angeles

3. Angels grabbing the legs of ***chicks*** flying overhead = Chicago

4. ***Philadelphia*** cream cheese smothered on the chicks' heads = Philadelphia

5. A ***car*** (manufactured in Detroit) spinning its wheels in that cheese = Detroit

6. A huge cable, complete with ***cable cars***, attached to the car = San Francisco

7. ***Washing*** hanging all along the cables = Washington

8. A Quebecer painting Canadian flags on the washing = Montreal

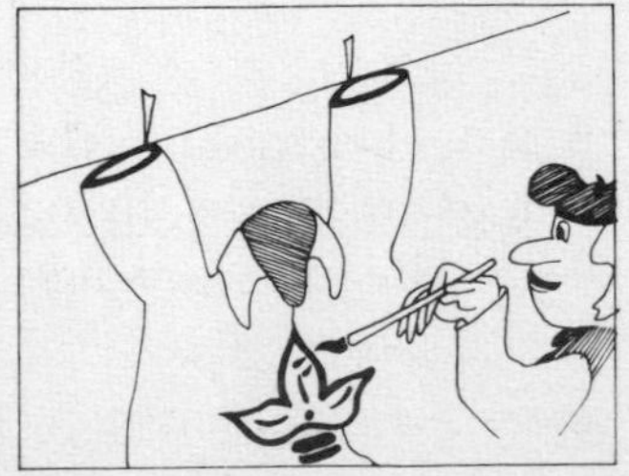

9. The needle-like ***C.N. Tower*** piercing those flags = Toronto

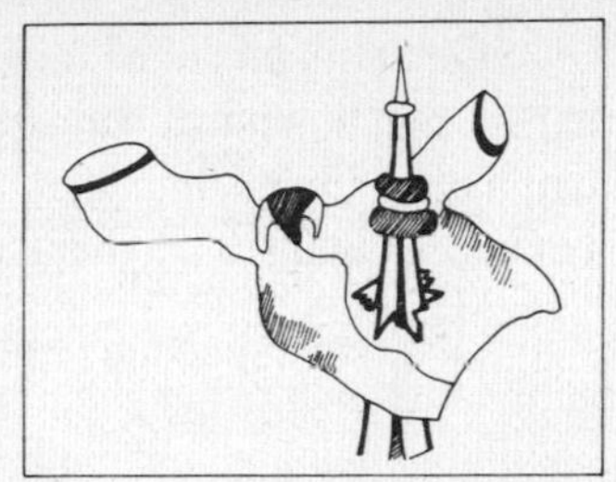

10. ***Boston baked beans*** being dumped on the C.N. Tower = Boston

Still have your mind pictures intact? Good. Continue. But be more vivid in your images. If they're yours, they'll be even easier to remember. Those Boston baked beans are exploding, and ***pits*** are flying out of them. ***Pittsburgh. Joe Louis,*** complete with boxing gloves, is socking away at those pits as they pop loose. ***St. Louis.*** Suddenly Joe Louis is run over by a stampeding football team – the ***Baltimore Colts. Baltimore.*** A huge building called ***Cleveland House*** smashes down on the team, crushing them. ***Cleveland.*** (If you're not familiar with the Cleveland House resort, be sure to use something else.) A western singer is perched on top of Cleveland House singing a song called ***"Houston." Houston.*** As he sings, a brand ***new ark*** comes floating by. ***Newark.*** What's on the ark? Why ***Minnie*** Mouse, singing and dancing. ***Minneapolis.*** And people are pelting her with huge rag ***dolls. Dallas.*** They're talking dolls. In fact screaming dolls. And one of them is screaming "My name's ***Anna.***" ***Anaheim.*** And as she screams her name, she jumps into the ***sea. Seattle.***

Get the picture? You are telling a story in your mind with visual images. You can see the plot unravel. One incident leads to the other. Let's review this part of the story:

11. The Boston baked beans are exploding and ***pits*** are popping out = Pittsburgh

12. Joe ***Louis*** the boxer is slugging those pits = St. Louis

13. The ***Baltimore*** Colts football team tramples Joe Louis = Baltimore

14. ***Cleveland*** House plumps right on top of the football team = Cleveland

15. A westerner sings "***Houston***" while sitting atop the building = Houston

16. A ***new ark*** floats past the singer = Newark

17. ***Minnie*** Mouse is dancing atop the ark = Minneapolis

18. Fans are pelting rag ***dolls*** at Minnie = Dallas

19. One of the dolls yells that her name's ***Anna*** = Anaheim

20. The doll called Anna jumps, screaming, into the ***sea*** = Seattle

You can continue your story. The sea turns out to be made of beer, the beer that made ***Milwaukee*** famous. And it starts to rain ***sen sen (Cincinnati),*** making the sea overflow into the ***Atlantic*** Ocean ***(Atlanta)***. Suddenly there is the ***patter, patter (Patterson)*** of hoofs and along comes a herd of buffalo ***(Buffalo)*** running across the water. So you have the last five cities for review:

21. The sea consists of ***beer*** that made Milwaukee famous = Milwaukee

22. It starts to rain ***sen sen*** (breath fresheners) which pelts against the sea = Cincinnati

23. The sea overflows into the ***Atlantic*** Ocean = Atlanta

24. Suddenly comes the ***patter*** of hoofs = Patterson, N.J.

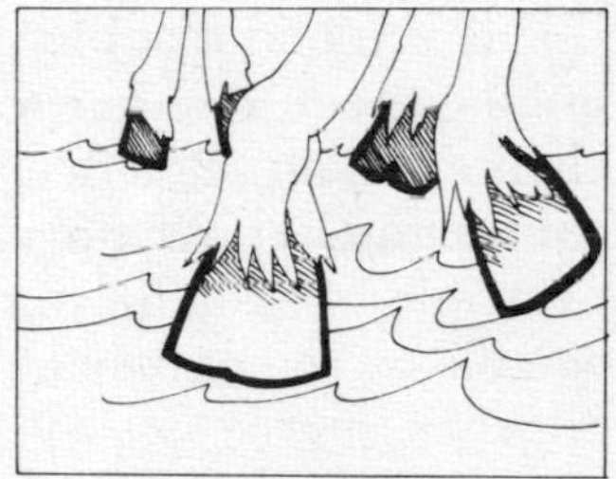

25. And a herd of ***buf-falo*** stampedes across the ocean = Buffalo

If you've done your best to visualize those pictures, you should now be able to take paper and pen and write out the twenty-five largest cities in order of descending population, by memory, without referring to this book. Review them again. Then forget about it until you finish the book. A few hours from now – or a few days from now – you should still be able to recall the list. In fact, I doubt whether you'll be able to ***forget*** it.

For you have followed the rules for accurate recall. You have paid attention and ***visualized*** the cities. By attempting to visualize them and link them together you have transferred them to long-term storage. And by remembering them in an organized manner, with clues for recall, you are able to remember them at will.

You should be proud of yourself. Who said you had a poor memory? I'll bet you can startle your friends by rhyming off the twenty-five largest cities. But don't rhyme off the pictures in your mind. They'll think you're looney.

If you had trouble visualizing those scenes and linking them together to form a story, go over this chapter again. Practice forming those picutres in your mind. You'll do it. And by using this same principle of visualization and association, you will be able to remember almost anything. In ***and*** out of order.

Read on and see how.

Chapter 6

Using Memory Pegs

In Order To Remember

The only weakness of the link system demonstrated in chapter 5 is that you cannot state the 12th largest city without mentally rhyming off the first eleven.

If it's important to recall material by number, simply commit a series of "pegs" to memory. Let "one" be represented by some object, "two" by another and so on. Then, instead of associating the list of items with each other, simply associate them with their corresponding numbers.

Let's see how it works. First, decide how many items you think you'll have to remember at any one time. There's no sense in memorizing one hundred peg words if you'll only need twenty or thirty. I found that twenty pegs were about all I needed. With twenty pegs I am able to remember a shopping list, points of a speech, facts from a magazine article, items discussed at meetings. I have no necessity, nor desire, to commit a fifty-six page magazine to memory or to remember seventy-five grocery items.

But if I'm without a pen and paper and need to remember a series of points until I get back to my office or home, there's no problem with twenty pegs committed to memory.

Let's assume twenty is sufficient for your needs as well. Now visualize something that you can easily associate with the number 1. It can be a wand or a walking stick or a carrot because these objects actually resemble a 1.

I'll list the images I have chosen. Some of them were taken from books on memory. Others I chose myself. Do the same. If you have a baby who just celebrated his or her first birthday, visualize a baby to represent 1. Pick something that is easy for ***you*** to commit to memory. The more personal – the more meaningful to you – the easier it will be to remember them.

1. Wand: I visualize a dainty fairy god-mother wearing army boots waving this sparkling wand over the object to be remembered, changing it in some way.

2. Swan: A swan is shaped like the number 2. I visualize a huge, beautiful white swan swimming in a lake.

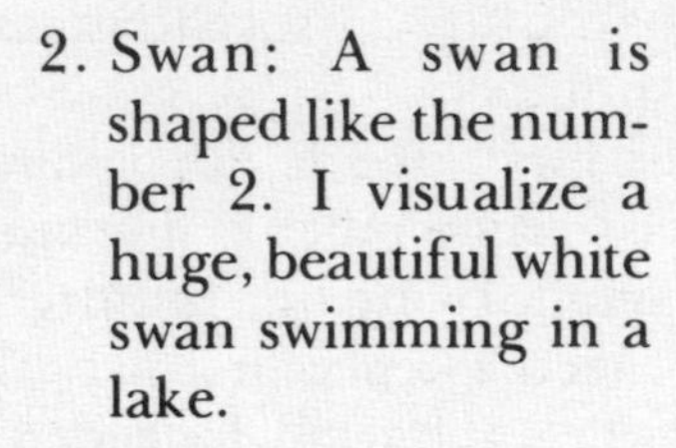

3. Clover: A 3-leaf clover. I usually see an animated clover – with eyes, mouth, arms – the works!

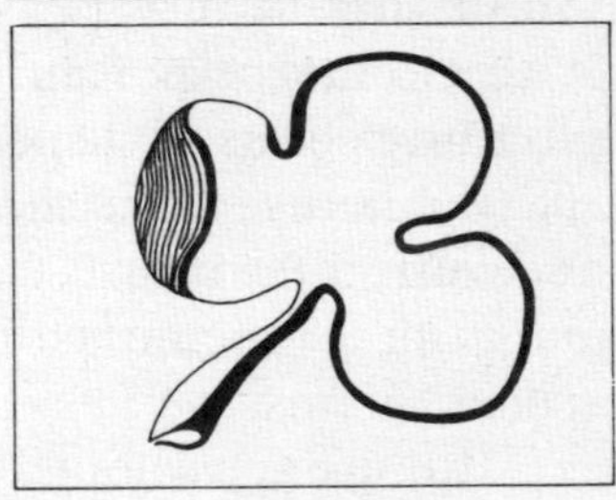

4. Chair: It has 4 legs. I usually see the chair coming to life as well. Depends upon the object I'm associating with it.

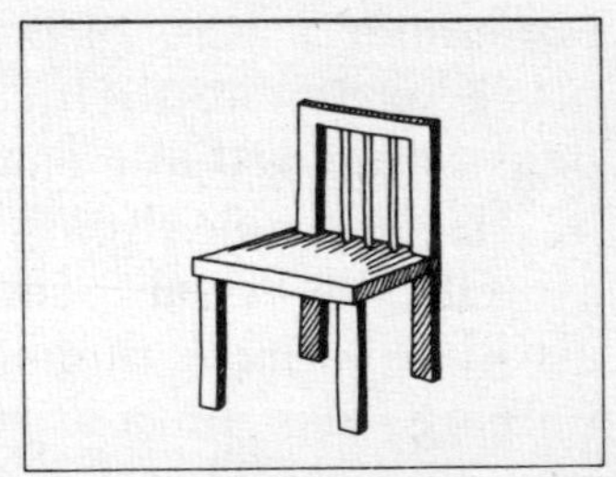

5. Star: Has 5 points. Sometimes I see a star-fish. Sometimes a star in the sky. Whatever forms a ridiculous association with the item I'm trying to remember.

6. Elephant: His trunk is shaped like the number 6. And an elephant can do some weird, wonderful things.

7. Pick: A pick looks like a 7. I get action into my picture. It's always digging at the item I'm remembering.

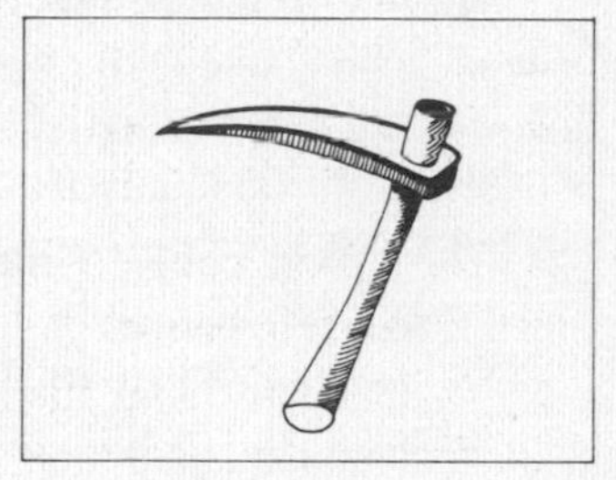

8. Figure skater: Because of the figure 8s most skaters perfect. I usually visualize the item I want to recall skating around the rink.

9. Pipe: A pipe looks like the figure 9 on it's back. I usually have somone smoking the item in a pipe. Or someone smoking the item instead of a pipe.

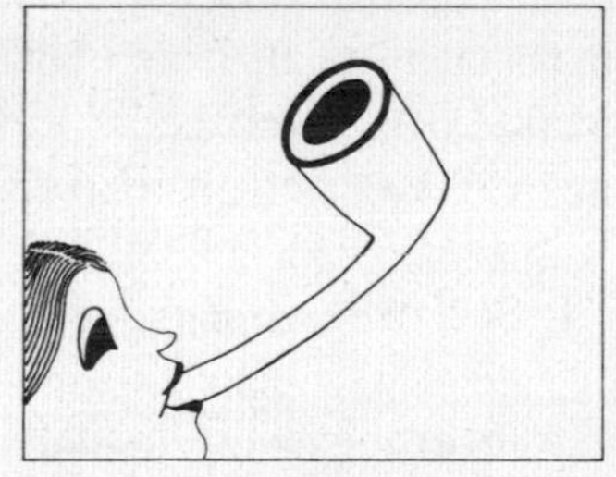

10. Potatoes: This is personal. As a kid I always used to have to lug home 10 lbs. of potatoes. A lot of action can be obtained with an unlimited supply of potatoes.

Now take a minute and commit these symbols to memory. If you find it difficult to associate mine, choose your own. Review them a few times. It should only take about ten minutes to commit them to memory. Write them out. Repeat them aloud. What's number 4? Right, a chair with 4 legs. What's number 8? What's number 7? Test yourself.

Have you memorized them? Okay, then let's see how we can use them. Suppose you had to remember a shopping list as follows:

1. 1 pkg. cooked ham
2. one dozen eggs
3. one quart of milk
4. five lbs. of bananas
5. four rolls of toilet paper
6. 1 box laundry detergent
7. 1 bottle ketchup
8. 1 watermelon
9. 1 tin of salmon
10. 1 lb. of butter

To remember the list by this method you would associate each item with its corresponding peg. Make your picture as ridiculous as possible. Exaggerate. Get action into the scene. For example:

1. See the ***wand*** (wielded by a fairy godmother) being waved over a pig (which represents ham). The pig immediately grows to be ten feet tall.

2. See a whole flock of ***swans*** scattering madly about a lake as they are pelted with eggs. Visualize those eggs breaking, and yolks dripping down the swans' necks and backs.

3. Picture a bunch of animated ***clovers*** diving into a bathtub full of milk. See them splashing and swimming – and drinking.

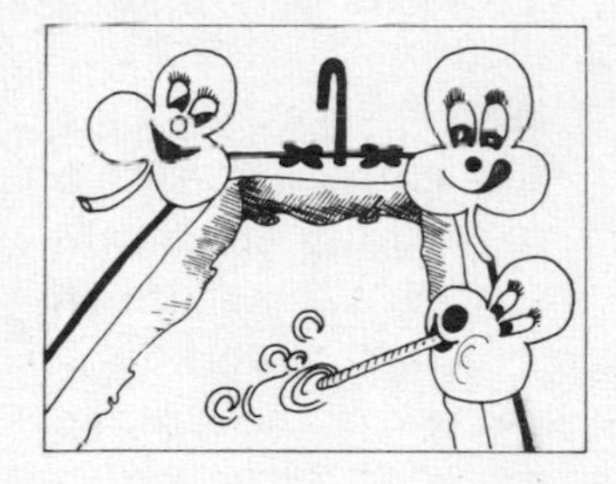

Let's pause for a minute. You'll notice we are simply trying to associate the item, not the quantity. Your natural memory will provide the details. When you think of number ***3***, you're reminded of the peg word ***clover.*** And you can see the bunch of clovers diving into a tub of milk and swimming like crazy. When you've identified the item as ***milk,*** your natural memory will tell you it's ***one*** quart, not two or three quarts.

4. Picture in your mind a herd of chairs running around eating bananas. Have them slip and slide on the banana peels that they toss on the ground; get action into your picture.

5. Visualize toilet paper strung from star to star in the sky – like decorations on a Christmas tree. Or, if it seems more ridiculous, picture a roll of toilet paper on top of a Christmas tree instead of the usual star.

6. Picture an ***elephant*** washing its clothes with a scrubbing board. Soap bubbles are everywhere.

7. Imagine someone smashing hundreds of bottles of ***ketchup*** with a pick. See that red, messy ketchup splashing all over the place.

8. A ***watermelon*** is skating on a rink doing figure eights. Better still, visualize dozens of watermelons doing figure eights.

9. Someone is smoking a ***salmon*** – in his pipe! You can smell the fishy aroma. Ugh!

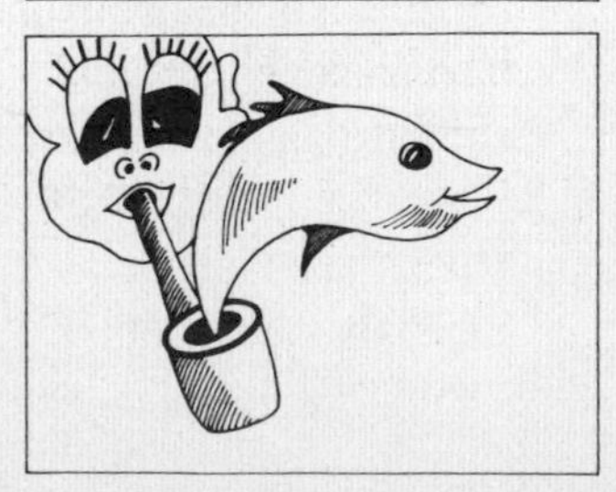

10. These cute little potatoes with dozens of eyes are running down the street – chased by a potato masher. They keep slipping in gobs of ***butter*** as they try to escape.

If you have made an honest effort to see these scenes in your mind's eye, you should have no trouble reciting that grocery list forward or backwards – or in any order. It would be even ***easier*** if you had made up your own scenes.

If you're asked for item 6, you see that elephant doing his laundry and you know the item is laundry detergent. If you're asked what number 4 is, you should be able to see those chairs eating bananas and slipping on the peels – telling you it's bananas. Oh yes, five pounds.

Try them all, from 1 to 10, without looking at the book. Can you get them all? If you can, you're home free. Now you can use the same peg words for any other list. And when you use it again, the original list will disappear from your mind and be replaced by the new list. It's like a self-erasing tape!

You can use the peg system instead of the link system if you have to recall specific items, by number, quickly. Otherwise the link system is sufficient.

In the next chapter we'll commit another ten pegs to memory. But this time we'll illustrate how they can be used to remember lists of things to do.

Chapter 7

Remembering Your "Things To Do" List

From Sentences To Pictures

Do you ever get an idea while driving the car or think of two or three things you'd like to do when you get back to the office or home – only to find you forget them later? Unless you always carry a pen and paper at your side, even at bedtime, this is probably a common occurrence. By applying the peg system, you can remember as many "things to do" as you have pegs. But first, let's memorize a few more peg words.

11. Picket Fence: 11 extended to 11111 etc. resembles a picket fence. I see a white fence with pointed pickets.

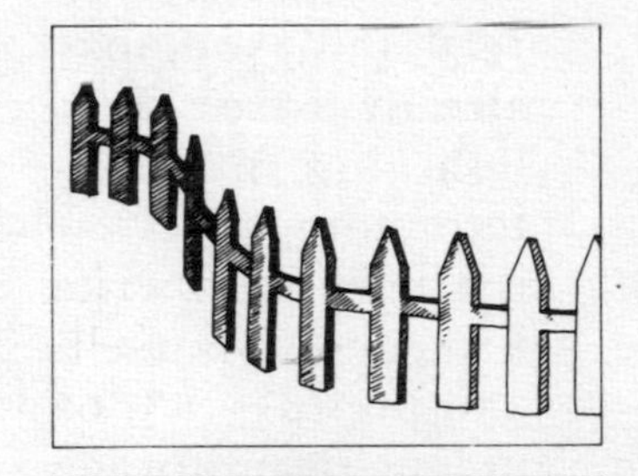

12. Clock: Since 12 o'clock is familiar and a popular time. I visualize a large round wall clock.

13. Black Cat: Since black cats and 13's are both bad luck. Make it a large, fuzzy one.

14. Lightning: I had difficulty associating this one too. But I tried so hard I couldn't forget it. Lightning flashing across the sky is supposed to resemble the number 14. Substitute something else if you like. But by the time you read this, you may already have 14 = lightning in short-term storage. Review it a few times, write it out, test yourself, and presto – it'll be in long-term storage as well.

15. Elevator: Not a good association. If you have a meaningful one, use it. But an elevator stopping at the fifteenth floor is as good as any.

16. Pretty Girl: I couldn't help thinking of "sweet sixteen" so I selected a pretty girl to represent the number 16.

17. Dancing: It's personal. I attended my first "prom" at age 17. So I visualize a young couple – or the items to be remembered – dancing.

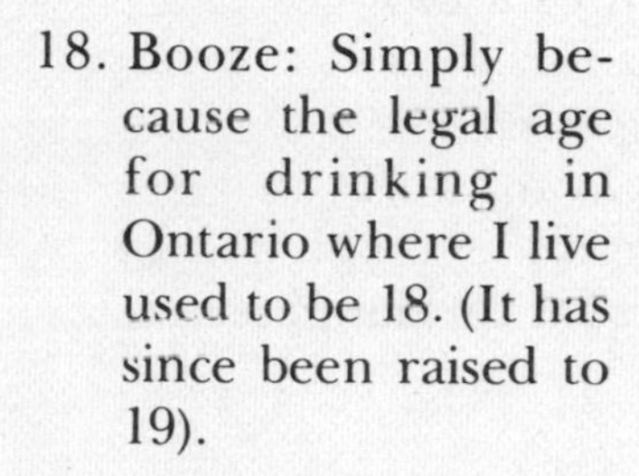

18. Booze: Simply because the legal age for drinking in Ontario where I live used to be 18. (It has since been raised to 19).

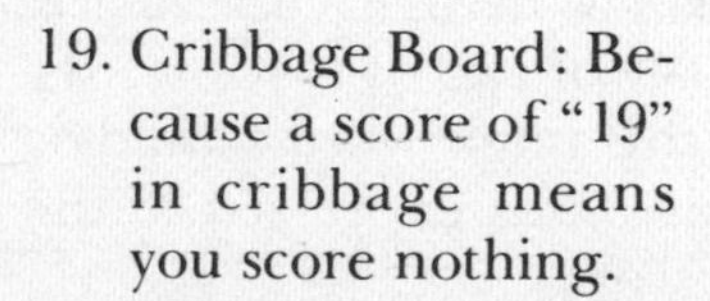

19. Cribbage Board: Because a score of "19" in cribbage means you score nothing.

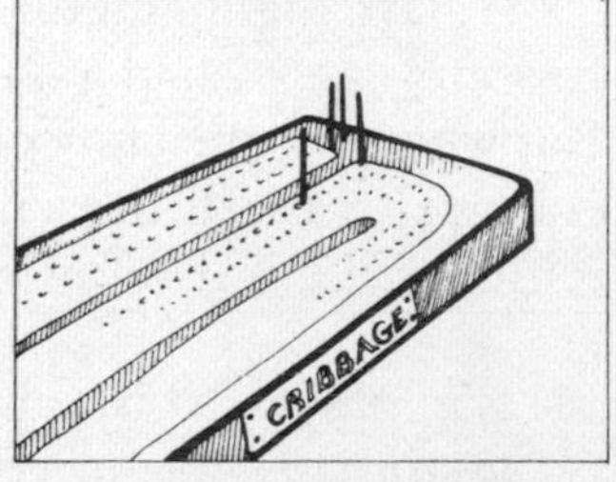

20. Horn of Plenty: I use this from a sound-alike peg system that I once learned from a Dale Carnegie course. It stuck in my mind over the years: twenty – horn of plenty.

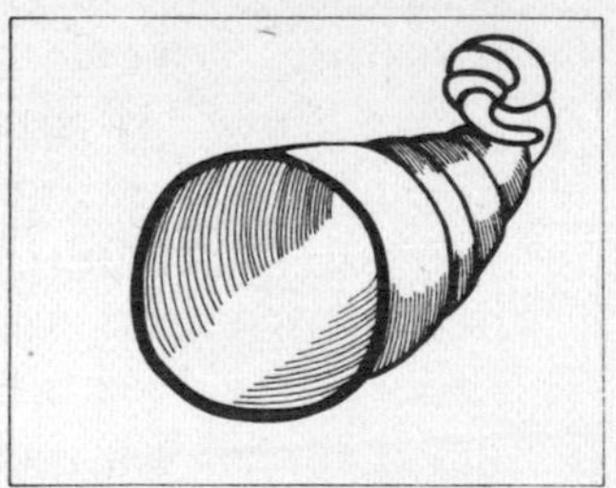

Now review these pegs from 11 to 20. Repeat them to yourself. Write them down. Try to ***visualize*** the peg words each time. Actually ***see*** that picket fence or black cat or horn of plenty. Don't read any further until you are sure you have memorized them.

Okay, let's assume you had a long drive to work and you thought of the following things you had to do that day:

11. Phone Mr. ***Mayer***
12. Look up article on ***stress*** in the paper
13. Write a memo to staff re ***Christmas*** Party
14. Return books to the ***library***
15. Order new ***carpet*** for office
16. Pay invoice for ***typewriter***
17. Make out ***paychecks*** for staff
18. Set up appointment to see Bob ***Willson***
19. Buy ***birthday*** present for daughter
20. Get a ***haircut***

I have highlighted a key word in each sentence. In some cases I had a choice of two or three words. But whatever the choice, this single word should be enough to recall the entire idea expressed in the sentence. Let's see how it works.

11. For ***Mayer,*** you can visualize a mare jumping over a ***picket fence.*** If she doesn't make it and you see that mare being impaled on the fence, you'll never forget it.

Can you visualize it? Have you associated the mare with the picket fence? Good. When you want to recall number 11, think of the key for 11 – picket fence. The picket fence will bring the picture to mind. You'll see the mare jumping the fence. And "mare" will remind you that you are to phone Mr.

Mayer. All your mind needs is a clue. You'll know you have to ***phone*** Mr. Mayer, not write to him or visit him. Let's commit the balance of your "things to do" list to memory. With practice you can do it very quickly.

12. Now we have to associate ***stress*** with a ***clock,*** representing number 12. How about visualizing a clock under stress. Actually see those hands quivering, the frame shaking, the face breaking out in a sweat. Always remember that the more ridiculous or preposterous a picture is, the more easily it will be retained in your mind.

Now when you think of the number 12, it should immediately remind you of a clock. Think about that clock, and you will see it, shaking under great stress. Stress will remind you to look up the article on stress.

13. I picked the key word, ***Christmas.*** So visualize a Christmas tree if you like. See a bunch of ***black cats*** (number 13) climbing all over it, knocking off the ornaments and making a terrible mess. When you ask yourself what was the 13th thing you had to do, you think of the number's representative, black cat. Then you can see in your mind's eye what that

cat is doing – with dozens of other cats – clawing at your beautiful Christmas tree. The clue will be enough to recall that you have to write a memo to the staff about the Christmas party.

14. Associate the word ***library*** with the symbol for number 14 – ***lightning.*** Visualize a storm ***inside*** the library. Thunder, rain, lightning, the works! The books are getting soaked and librarians are scurrying for cover. It's so ridiculous that as soon as your mind thinks of number 14 and converts it to lightning, the scene comes to view. And the association with the library is enough to recall that you have to take the books back to the library.

15. Number 15 is ***elevator.*** So how about dozens of rolls of ***carpets*** popping out of the elevator as soon as the doors open? If you can get ***yourself*** into the picture, and have those carpets crash down on top of you, the image will be even easier to recall. This is true for any of the scenes we have pictured to date.

Just a quick review of how to convert a word to a picture, in case you're having difficulty. Remember to exaggerate – make the picture ridiculous in some way. Like rain in a library. Or a clock under stress. See a lot of the objects. Like dozens of carpets or cats! Add action. A mare (or dozens of mares) jumping. Cats clawing. Carpets popping. Put yourself in the picture if you can. Make the items you are trying to recall larger than normal, or unusual in color or appearance. Animate them if you can – make them come alive. You don't ***have to*** do all this. But if you do, it will be so implanted in your memory you will not be able to ***prevent*** it from popping into your mind at the mere mention of its corresponding number, or peg.

16. The first impulse might be to visualize a ***pretty girl*** using a ***typewriter.*** Don't do it! It's too common. It makes sense. And it won't remain in your memory as easily. If you want to have a pretty girl running around the office throwing huge orange typewriters at the other employees, okay. Or if you want to see a pretty girl being rolled into a typewriter like a piece of paper and someone typing on her face, that might be even better.

Use the techniques referred to in the previous paragraph when you are forming your own word pictures. Effective images are usually humorous. You should have fun inventing a hilarious scene. And you won't easily forget it. What's number 16? A pretty girl. Typewriter. Pay the invoice for the typewriter. It should be as simple as that.

17. Seventeen is a couple ***dancing.*** And ***paycheques*** can be represented as money. If you like you can have two twenty dollar bills dancing with each other. Or have a couple dancing on a bed of money, with dollar bills raining all over them. Get something unusual into the picture. And action. What's 17? Money – paycheques. Make out paycheques for the staff.

18. ***Booze.*** Associate it with ***Willson*** in some ridiculous way. To do this you have to pick something to represent Willson. ***Wills*** is close enough. If you visualize a drunk making out his "will" and he's slopping booze all over it – perhaps even dipping his pen in booze instead of ink, that'll do it. Think of 18, booze. And you'll be reminded of the drunk making out his will – ***Willson.*** Oh yes, set up an appointment to see Bob Willson.

19. Be careful of this one. Visualizing your daughter receiving a cribbage board for her birthday might not be weird enough to stick in your mind. Better visualize a

birthday cake with flaming ***cribbage*** boards instead of candles. Complete with someone – your daughter preferably – trying to douse the flames with a seltzer bottle.

20. A ***horn of plenty*** lends itself to things falling out of it, like the elevator (number 15). But get action into it. And quantity. Perhaps hundreds of ***hair*** pieces (or toupees) tumbling out of a horn of plenty, and burying you alive. You can feel the hair getting into your mouth. Can you recall the sensation? Yuk. If you add this little touch of tasting, feeling, you'll have no trouble remembering what it is that is pouring out of that horn of plenty.

This applies to any of your mental pictures. Try to include ***sensation***. Feel the pain, roughness, gooeyness, wetness, or whatever sensation is elicited by the action depicted. It will help cement it into your long-term storage.

Okay, if you were able to imagine the above scenes – actually see them in your mind's eye – you shouldn't even have to review them. What's number 12? That's right a clock. And it's under obvious stress. Look up the article on stress. What's number 14? Lightning. A storm in the library. Take the books back to the library. Number 16? A pretty girl. The typewriter. Pay the invoice for the typewriter. And number 19? A cribbage board – birthday cake – buy a birthday present for your daughter.

What are the other ones? Number 11? How about 13? What does 15 bring to mind? Number 20? You not only know the list of things to do, but you can call them out by number – in and out of order. Even backwards.

And you can use these same word pegs to remember a sales presentation, a speech, facts for exams, for any series of items you may want to recall later.

But what happens when you want to use these same pegs for a completely different purpose? Will number 11 always bring back an image of a mare jumping the fence? The answer is no. It will only remain in your memory until you re-use the pegs. Then the first images are wiped out completely, and replaced by the new ones. It's like a self-erasing tape. Try it on ten completely different objects and see for yourself. The peg system is an excellent way to remember items that you will shortly be recalling. But you will want to re-use the pegs, so don't memorize items you want to retain forever, unless you have memorized plenty of pegs and won't need to re-use these same pegs again.

Instead, use the link system. With the link system you can memorize any number of different speeches and retain them forever.

In the next chapter, I'll show you how.

Chapter 8

Memorizing Jokes And Speeches

From The Mind To The Mouth

The best way to memorize a speech is not to memorize it. Memorize an outline instead. Then let your pre-determined thoughts run freely, lending spontaneity and enthusiasm to your speech. It's not only unnecessary to memorize a speech word for word, it's undesirable. One forgotten word or phrase and you stumble and falter. Assume you want to deliver the following brief speech entitled "How to Speak in Public."

HOW TO SPEAK IN PUBLIC

If you want to become a successful public speaker there are four points that you must always keep in mind.

1. ***Be prepared.*** The biggest fault of many accomplished speakers is that they get lazy. They feel they no longer have to prepare – and their lack of preparation is usually obvious. Your audience deserves your best; don't cheat them. If you're not an accomplished speaker, it's even more important to spend ample time in preparation. Lack of preparation aggravates stage frights. You should always know more about your topic than you'll ever have time to tell.

2. ***Organize your talk.*** Every speech or presentation should have an objective. Write it down. Are you trying to inform, persuade or entertain? Then write out the entire speech. Read it to yourself. Be familiar with the ideas. But don't memorize it. Memorized speeches are not spontaneous. It becomes a performance. An act. You appear to be talking at your audience, not with them.

The same thing applies to reading a speech.

In fact the audience may feel it's worse. They may feel insulted that you didn't think them worthy of a prepared speech. If you must read a speech, be familiar enough with your material that you can look around leisurely and comfortably, imitating "first-time utterance." Rehearse it to perfect your timing, pauses, inflections and change of pace.

A better method than reading the speech or memorizing it in its entirety is to write it out, give each new idea a heading and memorize the headings or key words of each heading.

3. ***Watch your delivery.*** Don't start by thanking the chairman. Instead, make a casual reference to something he said or a comment on the previous speaker. Acknowledge your audience. Don't tear right into your speech. Pause a moment to look at them and begin with a sentence that indicates you are aware they are there. Be enthusiastic. Enjoy yourself. Exude confidence. Don't fidget or pace. Speak naturally but with enough volume that everyone can hear you. Gesture if it's natural to you. In fact the key to a successful speech is being natural in your delivery. Don't try to be a comedian – unless you are one. Humor must be relevant. Avoid hackneyed expressions, jargon and pompous words. Everyone loves sincerity and hates a phony.

And make your ending neat and prompt. It's better for an audience to think, "What? It's over so soon?" than "Oh no, is he never going to quit?"

4. ***Overcoming stage fright.*** Experiencing a little stage fright every time you appear before an audience is normal. In fact, it's desirable – it helps us to do our best. We are naturally concerned about how we will come across, and we want to do a good job. A little stress never hurt anyone – especially when we have

the opportunity to work it off through the activity of delivering a talk or making a presentation. But we should never allow our stage fright to become out and out fear. It not only disrupts the talk, it disrupts the audience as well. If you're nervous, they're nervous. It's contagious.

To keep stage fright under control, concentrate on your message, not on yourself. Talking to twenty, fifty or one hundred people is no different than talking to two or three – with the exception of having to talk a little louder. We would have no difficulty jumping a four foot wide stream, but a similar gap thousands of feet high on a mountain cliff can immobilize us with fear if we allow ourselves to think of the height. So don't. Concentrate on the jump – or the speech.

Remember

Be prepared.
Organize your talk.
Watch your delivery.
And overcome stage fright.

If you keep these four points in mind, you'll soon be on your way to becoming a successful public speaker.

After writing out the speech and becoming familiar with every thought you want to express, make an outline of the key points as follows:

HOW TO SPEAK IN PUBLIC

1. BE PREPARED
   - lazy
   - stage fright
   - more than necessary

2. ORGANIZE
   - objective
   - write it out
   - don't memorize it
   - don't read it
   - headings only

3. DELIVERY
   - start slowly
   - enjoy yourself
   - don't be a comedian
   - end promptly

4. OVERCOME STAGE FRIGHT
   - a little stress is good
   - control fear
   - concentrate on message

Next, key your main points into the first four peg words in Chapter 6.

Wand. See a fairy godmother running around a huge restaurant preparing meals with a tap of her wand. She touches a plate and "poof" – pheasant under glass.

A tap on another plate and "presto" – instant roast beef and yorkshire pudding. Get the idea? When you stand in front of an audience and deliver your opening sentence (It's okay to memorize the opener) you think of number 1 – wand – and you see the fairy godmother preparing instant meals. This is enough to remind you that the first keypoint in delivering a speech is preparation. You may want to adlib everything under this first heading. And if you're familiar with your material you'll have no trouble doing that. But if you want to make sure you don't overlook a point, link the various points to the initial heading using the "link" or "story" system (see Chapter 5).

So your memory link may go something like this. The wand-wielding fairy godmother ***prepares*** meals. The meals are left uneaten because people are too ***lazy*** to eat them. So she jumps up and down, frightens them and they start eating like crazy, gobbling up ***more than necessary.***

Now let's see how your mind would operate on stage. "The first point to keep in mind is to be ***prepared***." Then your mind sees those meals sitting idle because people are too ***lazy*** to eat them. "The biggest fault of many professional speakers is the fact that they get lazy." Notice you probably won't use the same words as you had written down. But who cares? Explain what would happen if speakers were too lazy to prepare properly. When you've said all you know, think about what happened next after the people were too lazy to eat. Oh yes, the fairy godmother ***frightened*** them. So tell the audience the lack of preparation can also cause stage fright. Tell them why. Don't worry about using the exact words. You ***know*** why. If you're not knowledgeable about your subject you wouldn't be addressing the group in the first place. When you've told the audience about stage fright, think of your story again. Oh yes, when she frightened them, they ate

more than necessary. That's enough to remind you to tell the audience to know more about your topic than necessary.

Get the idea? Crazy picture stories in your mind won't fade under stress. In fact you won't be under stress because you'll be confident that you have your memory clues to fall back on. The result will probably be that you don't ***need*** your clues. Because, hopefully you ***are*** knowledgeable in the area, and familiar with what you have written.

Build mental pictures for the other main points as well. Thus, point number 2 is represented by "swan" which you could have visualized playing an ***organ*** to remind you of "organized." Number 3, clover, you animate and have ***delivering*** the mail. Number 4, chair, could be on stage making a speech and skaking with ***fear***. Link the sub-headings to these key words to form a story, similar to the way we did for the first point "Be prepared."

Use your own imagination. Form your own associations and picture stories. You'll never have to pause or stammer trying to recall your next point. And at the end of the speech you can repeat those 4 main points by once again calling upon your "wand," "swan," "clover" and "chair."

Jokes can be remembered the same way. If you want to remember a series of jokes on different topics, simply number the topics and tie in the jokes, using the link or story technique. For example:

	TOPIC	JOKE
1.	Children	My son's so ill-tempered we have to put a pork chop around his neck before the dog will play with him
2.	Secretary	Gladys can't spell, which makes her inability to type a real asset
3.	Memory	"Doctor you've got to give me something to help my memory. It's terrible." "How long have you had this problem?" "What problem?"
4.	Inflation	If you want the will to live, just ask the price of a funeral

You can add as many topics as you have memory pegs. Then associate the topics with the peg words and link the joke to the topic. For example, since "one" is "wand," visualize that wand being waved over a crowd of children and see them disappear one at a time in a puff of smoke or see them grow to gigantic proportions, or float in the air in whatever makes a vivid image in your mind. Then associate children with the dog in the joke. Get the pork chop in your picture since it's essential to the joke. You might see children playing with pork chops as though they were dogs. See those pork chops jumping through hoops, racing across fields, barking at the children.

When you want to recall a joke about children, ask yourself "what are those children doing?" You'll see them playing with pork chops as though they were dogs. This will be enough of a clue to remind you of the joke. You can do the same with "secretary," "memory," and "inflation."

You don't ***need*** the peg words if you just want to recall the jokes by topic. But suppose you just want to remember a string of jokes for a party. In that case just run through your peg words one at a time and they'll remind you of the jokes. In the above example, the ***first*** joke you tell will be "wand" – "children" – "dog and pork chop" joke. When you're ready for the second joke, number 2 gives you "swan" and having associated the swan with secretary, you'll have the topic. Then thinking about the "secretary" will lead you to the scene associated with it – in this case spelling and a typewriter. Just as in speeches, don't try to memorize the joke word for word. Tell it in your own words. It's more effective that way.

Chapter 9

Overcoming Absentmindedness "It Slipped My Mind"

A Skid-Resistant Memory

Ever find yourself staring blankly into a filing cabinet drawer wondering what it is you were looking for? Or trying to recall where you put your spare pair of eyeglasses? Or searching in vain for your misplaced car keys? If so, you're no different from the rest of us; next to forgetting names, absentmindedness is the most common complaint of managers attending my memory training seminars. It ***can*** be overcome. But it requires a conscious effort. Even persons with excellent memories can be absentminded, for absentmindedness is nothing more than inattention. If you were not preoccupied with other thoughts and paid attention to where you put your spare pair of glasses, you would remember where they were.

We must educate ourselves to do things consciously and not to allow our thoughts to wander. The first step is to make up our minds right now that we are going to make the effort. We must convince ourselves that we ***want*** to recall where we left things and that we ***are*** going to recall where we left them. Then we can assist our ability to recall by making sure we have a vivid picture of where we put things.

This can be done in several ways. One is to have a ***reason*** for putting something where you do. Did you put your glasses in the top left-hand drawer of the kitchen cupboard because it's the closest one to the front door? Or in the medicine cabinet because that's where you keep your spare razor batteries, shoelaces, etc? If you have a logical reason for putting things where you do, you will probably be able to recall the ***reason*** which in turn will remind you of the ***place***.

Another way is to say it aloud. "I am putting the spare office keys in the top desk drawer because that's where the deposit box key is kept." Your brain listens to and remembers the sound of your voice.

To reinforce it even further, make a conscious association between the object and the place where you're placing it. For example, visualize that top drawer slamming shut on your glasses, smashing them into a thousand pieces. Get action into your picture. Exaggerate. The more ridiculous, violent, colorful visualizations are hard ***not*** to recall.

The very idea of making an association makes you think of what you're doing for at least a fraction of a second and that's usually all that's necessary. Remember, the eyes cannot see when the mind is absent.

Memory lapses sometimes result from concentrating too much on one thing and not enough on another. When we're thinking about that important visitor or catching a plane or giving a speech, we tend to forget the habitual things we do such as removing our eyeglasses and setting them on top of the filling cabinet or bookcase. But with a little willpower, we can get into the habit of making split-second associations.

If you bring a report with you when you go to lunch, and then set it on the chair, you can make sure you won't forget it by associating it with the check. Visualize the check with a report written on it in glaring red phosphorescent ink. Or visualize a huge report nailed across the exit blocking your way.

This may all sound ridiculous. It is. And that's why it works. And in time you will find you have acquired the habit of ***thinking about what you are doing.***

There's no easy way of curing absentmindedness. For it requires continuing attempts to be aware of what we are doing, of where we are putting things, or of things we are supposed to do, or of calls we are supposed to make. It's so easy to park the car and rush into the mall without paying one bit of attention to where we parked the car. It's easy because our mind is on our shopping or our time problem and not on the parking spot. Once we have acquired the habit of automatically picking out some landmark – a lamp post or flagpole for instance – and noting where our car is in relationship to it, it becomes easy to remember. Once we ***consciously*** make an association, it's easy to recall it later. And by now you should be getting better at making associations.

Chapter 10

"I Can't Remember Your Name"

What's His Name?

We all have trouble remembering names at one time or another. But those occasions can be reduced to a minimum if you conscientiously apply the suggestions contained in the previous chapters.

When you do have trouble remembering someone's name it's either because you don't hear it properly in the first place, or don't show sufficient interest to imprint the name into long-term memory storage. Or, you lack sufficient associative information to allow you to recall the name later.

To overcome the first two barriers, make up your mind now to be genuinely interested in people. Associate as many facts as possible with the people you meet. Repeat the name several times in the conversation. Try to visualize the face later. Practice the old A.I.R. formula (Attention, Interest and Repetition). For above all, you must ***want*** to remember. The brain is a miraculous piece of machinery. It senses your desire to remember, and transfers the information to long-term memory for future use.

To insure that you can recall the name later, take advantage of your natural powers of association. Just as the Statue of Liberty reminded you of the city, so a person's face can remind you of his or her name. And the method is the same.

Select a predominant feature of a person's face – the nose, lips, chin, eyes, etc. and mentally associate the person's name with that feature. Seeing the person's face at a later date – specifically that one feature – should allow you to recall the name by association. The feature reminds us of the name.

Here's an example. You meet someone called Billy Carswell. While you're talking to him you convert the name to something tangible. The name

"Billy" reminds you of ***billy-goat*** and "Carswell" breaks down into the objects ***cars*** and ***well***. You search his face for some outstanding feature and finally select the nose because it is slightly larger than normal. Now you draw a mental picture of a huge pink ***billy-goat*** tearing out of the nostrils and smashing into hundreds of yellow polkadot ***cars***, sending them careening into a wide bottomless ***well***. The point to keep in mind when forming your picture is to make it colorful, exaggerated and with plenty of action. The more striking, bizarre or absurd the association, the easier you'll remember it.

When you meet this person again, you search his face and ask yourself which feature you had selected. Oh yes, his nose. Now what was happening to that nose? Of course, a giant, colored ***billy-goat*** is charging out of the nostrils – the name is "Billy." And the goat is smashing into a bunch of cars, knocking them down a well. His name is "Carswell."

Sounds complicated. It's not, really – although some people find it difficult to convert the names to tangible objects or to select an outstanding feature. But in most cases, just the ***effort*** in trying to do so is sufficient. For you have paid attention. You have concentrated on the name and the face. They are imprinted indelibly in your long-term memory and need only a clue – an association – to be retrieved later.

Don't be discouraged if you have trouble picking a clue or symbol to represent the name. This will come with practice. And the clue does not have to be that good. If the name is "Henderson" simply visualizing a "hen" clawing at the person's bushy eyebrows will be enough of a clue. Once your mind gets the clue "hen," the whole name "Henderson" will be retrieved from your long-term memory storage.

Let's practice converting names to clues for recall. How would you ***visualize*** the following names?

Robbie McLeod
Donald Canning
Al Gunn
Mike Lemon
Lorena Pitt
David Stinson
Anne Smith
Doris Howard
Paul Crowley
Steve Best
Peter Armstrong
Bill Richard
Betty Coates
Mary Barclay
Bruce Jackson

Convert each name to something that sounds a little like the name. Something that you can visualize. Now I said that sounds a little like the name. Although most memory experts would have you take great pains in converting to identical "sound alikes," it's not necessary. For example, if you really thought about the first name for awhile, you could come up with four words, ROB, BEE, MACK AND LOUD, which would sound out the name exactly. Then you could build a word picutre such as a BEE ROBbing a MACK truck and yelling LOUDly as it makes it's escape. Of course you would have to search out a predominant feature of the person's face and link this picture to it.

It will work. No doubt about it. Except that it would take too long with more complicated names. The person would be long gone by the time you completed your word picture.

So keep it simple. Just visualize a ROBber yelling LOUDly. The important thing is to actually ***visualize*** it. Picture the robber with a black mask, or stocking over his face, pulling at the person's nose or trying to steal an ear. Try to associate the robber with the feature that seems to stand out. If you have searched the face and nothing stands out, simply pick anything. The eyes. An ear. The hair. Eyebrows. It doesn't matter.

Reinforce your picture every chance you get. If you're meeting several people, take your time. Keep looking back at the people, you've just met. See that word picture you've drawn in your mind. The important thing is not the picture you create. The important thing is how hard you ***try.*** For if you try hard, you have forced yourself to really ***observe*** the person's face. And to ***hear*** the name. And to ***associate*** the name to the face.

Let's pick substitutes for some of the other names:

Donald Canning: How about ***Donald*** Duck sticking a ***can*** over some part of his face.

Al Gunn: ***Ale*** is close enough to Al. Perhaps a ***gun*** shooting ale into his ear.

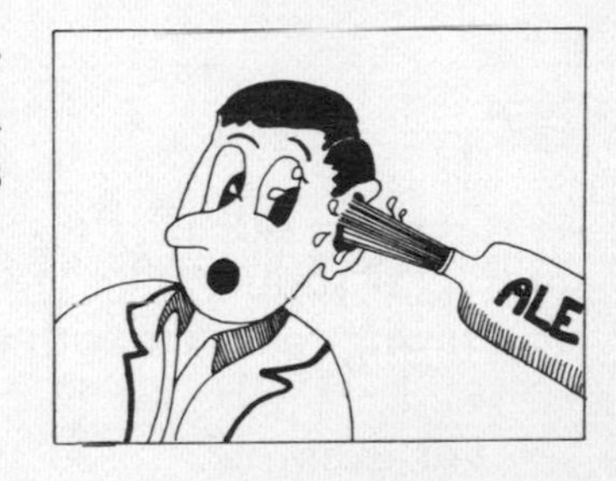

Mike Lemon: ***Microphone*** can be visualized for Mike. ***Lemon*** is great as it is.

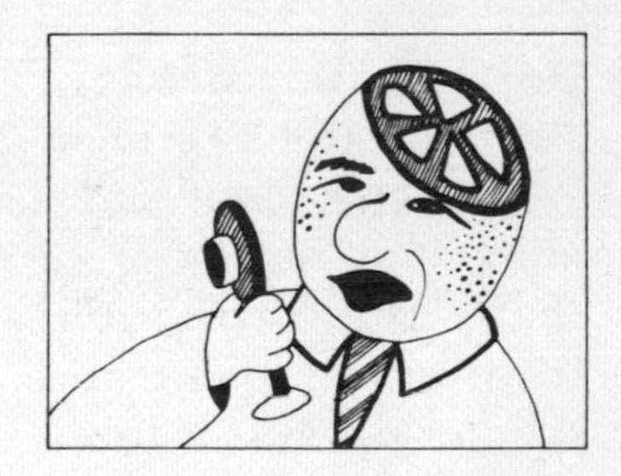

Lorena Pitt: ***Arena*** is close enough to Lorena. And a peach ***pit*** or snake ***pit***.

David Stinson: You could visualize a David as in David and Goliath. Have him wearing a big ***stetson***.

Anne Smith: Anne could be represented by an ant. Black***smith*** is okay for Smith.

Get the idea? Don't spend too much time finding a "sound alike" for the name. Spend more time trying to link it with the face.

For example:

Doris Howard: Right away you think of ***door.*** Picture that door slamming into her nose (if that's the prominent feature you pick) and splintering into a thousand pieces. Try to find a picture for ***Howard.*** If you can't, so what? Just try! And I'll bet when you recognize her as "Doris," the last name "Howard" will pop into your mind as well. (You could come up with an Indian saying "How!")

Paul Crowley: ***"Pull"*** is close enough to ***Paul.*** Visualize a ***crow*** being ***pulled*** out of a dimple or ear or whatever. Actually see it in your mind's eye.

If possible, make the picture ridiculous, colorful, loaded with action. The sillier it is, the more it will stick in your mind. With practice you will be able to do this with little effort. And you'll have plenty of opportunity to practice. You meet people all the time. Try this method with everyone you meet for the first time. Don't be discouraged if you fail at first. Keep trying. The effort will pay off.

How would you visualize the remaining names?

Steve Best
Peter Armstrong
Bill Richard
Betty Coates
Mary Barclay
Bruce Jackson

Whatever you picked to represent the names will be easier to remember than what I would have picked. Because ***you*** thought about it. ***You*** selected it. ***You*** were involved.

You think you have a bad memory for names? There's no such thing as a bad memory. You already have the ability. You have to use it. Start managing your memory. Now.

Chapter 11

How To Study

Being Put To The Test

Take advantage of your brain's associative powers. If you're studying over a period of time, always study in the same room, at the same desk or table. Then, when you're writing the exam, pretend you're in that same spot. You'll be amazed at how much more information you can recall. Most of the information will be associated in some way with your environment at the time you memorized the material. For instance, you may recall a song that was playing on a radio which in turn will remind you of a piece of information you were memorizing at that time. In some cases you may even be able to see the page in front of you.

However, you can utilize association to a greater extent than this. Use the same technique used in recalling the twenty-five largest cities, or names and faces.

For example, here are a few questions from one of my son's grade 9 tests. Follow along with me as we commit the answers to memory for easy recall later:

(1) What factors determine the strength of an electromagnet?
(2) Name six sources of electrical energy.
(3) What law describes the relationship between voltage, current and resistance in a circuit? Label the symbols.

Okay, let's take a look at the answers.

(1) The strength of an electromagnet is determined by:

(a) the amount of current
(b) the number of turns in a wire
(c) the size of the wire
(d) the type of material in the core

Now to associate these answers with the question, visualize this picture story in your mind. An electromagnet falls into a river and is swept away by the ***current.*** He flails frantically (animate your objects) but is swept around a ***turn*** in the river. He spots a ***wire*** hanging over the embankment. Grabbing hold of it he wraps it around his ***core*** to secure himself, and pulls himself ashore.

Now, when you're asked about the electromagnet, this scene should pop into your mind. The key words which we linked will provide your mind with a clue to recall the additional information. Can you ***see*** that electromagnet falling in the water and being swept away by the ***current?*** Then what is the first part of the answer? Right. ***The amount of current.*** Now what happens? Oh yes, he's swept around a ***turn*** in the river. The clue word ***turn*** tells you the next part of the answer: ***the number of turns in the wire.*** What happens

next? He spots a ***wire*** hanging over the embankment. That's the clue for the ***size*** of the wire. What does he do then? He grabs hold of the wire and wraps it around his ***core***. So the final part of the question is the ***type of material in the core.***

The more practice you get at visualizing these silly stories in your mind, the better – and faster – you become at it.

Now let's look at question (2). The six sources of electrical energy are:

(a) friction
(b) heat
(c) light
(d) chemicals
(e) pressure
(f) magnetism

Now, when I painted this picture in my son's mind, I used his kid brother as the first clue. Because he was always so active and full of ***energy.*** You should visualize someone ***you*** know to represent the electrical energy. But for now, let's say it's this little live wire of ours, Craig. And Craig is vigorously rubbing two pieces of metal together creating ***friction.*** He keeps going faster and faster, and the metal produces ***heat.*** Still he continues and the pieces of metal get red hot, giving off ***light.*** Faster and faster he rubs the pieces of metal together until they start to vaporize, emitting ***chemicals*** into the air. The chemicals fill the room, causing ***pressure*** to build up against the doors and windows. Finally Craig's mother releases the pressure by opening the doors and windows and gets rid of all the chemicals by attacting them with a huge ***magnet***.

Now, you're asked to name six sources of electrical energy. You visualize this energetic person rubbing something together to produce – ***friction***. He continues and it produces – ***heat***. Then ***light***. Finally it vaporizes forming – ***chemicals***. The chemicals build up, causing ***pressure***. And the pressure is relieved by getting rid of them with a huge ***magnet***. And there you have it. Review that mind picture a few times, and I guarantee you will get 100% on the test next week.

Don't worry if you have to stretch a point, exaggerate, or be inaccurate in order to form your picture story. The object is to get it into your long-term storage in such a way that it can be recalled later. For example, it would make more sense to have the metal vaporize to form a ***gas***, not ***chemicals***. But this inaccuracy only ***helps*** you to remember it.

The last question really forces you to use your imagination. It's not the easiest one to form a picture story with. But the greater effort required impresses it in your mind even more. So let's try it.

The law referred to is $1 = \frac{E}{R}$

where 1 = amps
E = volts
R = ohms

See if you can picture this. An ***Imp*** (elf-like creature?) is pole ***vaulting*** over the city of ***Rome***. And the crowd is yelling “Look at the ***Imp***! ***E’s vaulting*** over Rome!”

Imp will remind you of ***amp***. Vaulting will remind you of ***volts***. Rome will remind you of ***ohm***.

Can you reproduce the formula?

$$1 \text{ (amp)} = \frac{E \text{ (volts)}}{R \text{ (ohm)}}$$

Just visualize the picture of the Imp pole-vaulting over Rome, and hear the crowd yelling “look at the Imp, E’s vaulting over Rome!” when you’re asked question (3). Write it down. Then arrange it to form the proper equation, complete with symbols. These clues are sufficient to allow your mind to come up with the right equation and corresponding symbols. Try it.

There is nothing that you cannot commit to memory using these mind pictures. The effort of forming the mind pictures or picture stories will get the information into your long-term storage system. Then, visualizing these pictures later will allow you to recall the facts that they represent.

Studying can even be fun. Especially if you do it with a partner. It creates a lot of laughter. And two people brainstorming can come up with some pretty weird pictures. Pictures that you won't easily forget.

Chapter 12

How To Follow Directions

Getting From 'Hear' To There

Ever ask directions on how to get to a particular place and later find yourself hopelessly lost? Well you can use the link method to keep yourself on the right track.

But first, what if no street names are given? Many people can't remember street names – except perhaps the one they live on – so the directions you are given may sound like this:

"Just go straight ahead for three blocks. Then turn right. After about a mile or so you'll see an Esso service station on your right. Turn right at the station and go past two traffic lights. Just after the second traffic light, you'll see a huge television tower. Turn left just past that tower and keep going until you come to a fork in the road. Take the right fork, go about two miles and you'll see our house on the left-hand side. It's got a big stone gateway with a lion's head on each post."

In a case like this, try to put yourself into the picture. Pretend you are actually driving as the directions are given. Visualize passing three intersections. Actually ***see*** that Esso station. Feel yourself turning the wheel to the right as you sight that station. Actually ***see*** that television tower when you've passed two lights. Feel yourself turning the wheel to the left as you turn at the tower. See that fork in the road. Imagine yourself keeping to the right and driving until you see that big stone gateway on your left.

Ask the person to repeat the directions and take that mental trip again. When you actually ***do*** go there, it's almost like you've been there before. Because imagining you do something leaves almost as much of an imprint on your memory as actually doing it.

Now suppose you are actually given street names. Perhaps you've mapped out the route on a local street guide. But it's awkward, dangerous, and time consuming if you have to keep referring to a map as you drive. Simply commit the route to memory using the link system. Then visualize yourself driving the route as above.

Suppose someone explains how to get to 49 Turner Avenue:

"Take highway 401 to the Allen Expressway. Go south on the Allen Expressway to Eglinton Avenue. Turn west on Eglinton and keep going until you hit Oakwood. Turn south on Oakwood to St. Clair. Turn east on St. Clair and keep going until you reach Christie. Go south on Christie until you find Tyrrel. Turn west on Tyrrel and go a few blocks to Turner. Go south on Turner until you reach number 49 Turner Ave. It's a small white cottage."

With practice you will be able to convert the streets into mind pictures (the same way you handled names and faces) ***while the directions are being given.*** But it's safer to quickly write it down first. Then you can easily paint yourself a little picture story so you'll remember the directions.

Let's assume you're starting near Highway 401, so there's no problem remembering that part. But to remember it's the Allen Expressway turnoff, visualize an "allen key." This allen key is being thrust into an egg, smashing the shell. "Egg" will be sufficient to tell you it's Eglinton that you turn onto.

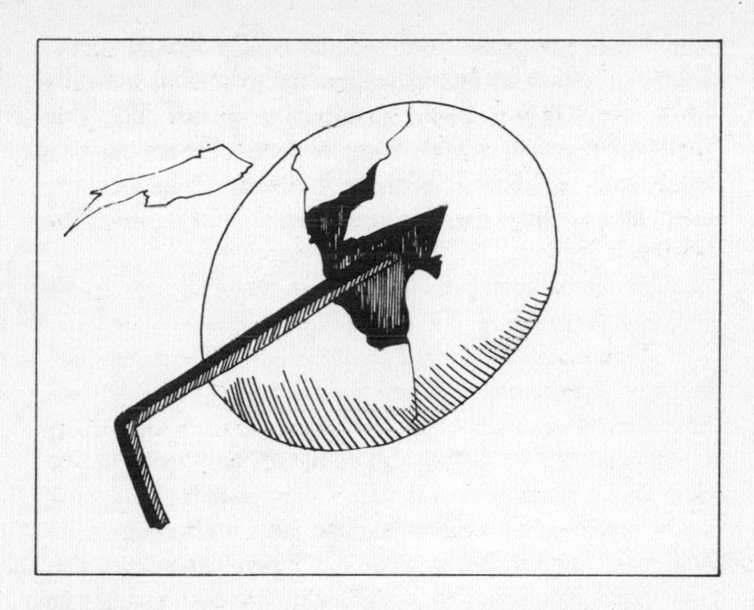

Now associate the egg with something. Let's picture the egg being smashed with an oak bat. See the action. Visualize the egg being splattered by that slab of oak. "Oak" is enough of a clue to remind you it's Oakwood.

Now you must associate Oakwood with the next street you take. Let's visualize that oak bat actually being transformed into a chocolate eclair. You bite into it. It's still hard, like wood, but it's full of chocolate sauce and whipped cream. The "eclair" will tell you the street is St. Clair.

What's happening to the eclair? Well, let's animate it and have it walk hand in hand with a cookie – that is, if you are familiar with the fact that Christie's make cookies. If not, use something else. (A "cross" for instance.)

The cookie is crying. See the "tears" dropping to the pavement, a clue that the next street is Tyrrel (pronounced tear-el).

Tyrrel

The tears are running down the street and "turn" the corner, reminding you that the next street is "Turner." The stream ends at a little white cottage – number 49. You can convert the number to an object as well. But you can't do that until chapter 13. So let's assume you've written the number down.

Sounds complicated, but it's not. A fast review of your fabricated scene, and you've committed the directions to memory – for easy recall days or even weeks later. To remember the east, west etc., simply convert them and turn left, or right, and visualize.

A fast review:

Go along 401 to the "Allen key" (Allen Expressway)

The allen key is smashing into an "egg" (Turn off at Eglinton)

The egg is being hit by an oakwood bat (Turn off at Oakwood)

The oakwood changes to an "eclair" (Turn off at St. Clair)

The eclair is walking with a "Christie" cookie (Turn off at Christie)

The Christie biscuit is crying "tears" (Turn off at Tyrrel)

The tears turn the corner (Turn off at Turner)

And the little white house where the stream ends is your number 49.

It's even easier to remember when you can build a little story. But linking unconnected words together works almost as well. I find the method extremely useful, even for the very simple directions such as "go along Burbanks to Forestgrove; turn right on Forestgrove and then turn left when you come to Page. Our house is number 35."

For this one, I visualize myself climbing up a bank, getting burrs all over me in the process (Burbank). I finally reach the top and, lo and behold, a huge forest (Forestgrove) is in front of me. So I make my way through the forest only to have a huge page (Page) from a book blocking my way.

Try it next time you're given directions. You'll be surprised at the results.

How do you remember the house number? The next few chapters will explain that.

How To Remember Numbers

The Numbers Game

If you have a natural memory for numbers, you may not need this. But most people, including myself, have trouble remembering telephone numbers, parking lot numbers, hotel room numbers, and the dozens of other numbers encountered on a daily basis. Eventually, through use, numbers will be transferred to your long-term memory storage system. But numbers used infrequently can take a long time – and cause a lot of inconvenience and frustration in the meantime.

Much of our trouble stems from the fact that we tend to over-estimate our ability to remember. If we're on a business trip for example, and we want to remember the mileage reading, we ***mentally*** record the last three digits, repeat them a few times to ourselves, and are satisfied that we can remember them. But four hours later, when we arrive at our destination, we are unable to recall them. They had only been in our short-term memory.

It's more difficult to get ***numbers*** into long-term memory storage since they form no visual images – no pictures – in our minds. How can we picture a "6" or a "24"? How can we associate a telephone number with a person?

What we must do first is change numbers into words. We already know we can recall words. Because words form pictures in our minds, and pictures enable association and instant recall. I bet you still know the largest cities in North America. The first one is New York since we can ***visualize*** the statue of liberty and ***associate*** it with the city. And we can visualize angels circling the outstretched arm, which gives us the second largest city, Los Angeles. And so on. Well we can do the same thing with numbers if we can first express them as meaningful words that can be visualized.

To do this, we must memorize a code. It may look difficult at first, but stick with it. It's no more difficult than the ten peg words you memorized earlier. I'll try to give you hints on memorizing them as we go along.

This code has every digit (from 0 to 9) represented by a phonetic sound. Here they are:

0 is represented by the sound of "s" or "z". You can remember by thinking of the word "zero."

1 is represented by the sound of "t", "d" or "th" – Think of "t" and "d" as having ***one*** downstroke.

2 is represented by the sound of "n" – Remember it because "n" has ***two*** downstrokes.

3 is represented by the sound of "m" – And "m" has ***three*** downstrokes.

4 is represented by the sound of "r" – You might remember it because the "r" is the last letter in "four."

5 is represented by the sound of "L" – Some experts suggest remembering it as the first half of 50, which in turn is represented by the "L" in Roman numerals. But if this seems too complicated, just memorize it by rote.

6 is represented by the sound of "j" or the similar sounds of soft "g" (as in gem), "ch" or "sh" – The written "j" does look like 6 in reverse, so you might remember it this way.

7 is represented by the sound of "k" or the similar sounds of hard "c" (as in cat) and hard "g" (as in go). There's no memory aid except that "7" looks something like a ***key***. If it helps, use it.

8 is represented by the sound of "f" or the similar sound of "ph" or "v" – To memorize it you might think of "f" as in fate (pronounced f-eight).

9 is represented by the sound of "p", the similar sound "b" – You can remember it because "p" looks like a mirror image of "9"

All the above sounds are consonants. Ignore all vowels, a, e, i, o, u, y and such letters as h and w. They will be used strictly as fillers, with no meaning.

Don't read any further until you have memorized the above code. Test yourself. What's number "7"? That's right, it's "k" or hard "g" of hard "c". Now what's number 9? Number 5? Study them until you know them in and out or order. Then read on!

Now for practice, let's convert a few simple numbers to meaningful words that you can visualize:

71 represents hard "c" sound plus a "d" or "t" sound. It can be represented by the word ***C****a****t*** or ***C****o****d*** or ***G****a****t****e* or ***G****oa****t***. There are dozens of words you could pick. Remember, vowels don't mean anything – they're only fillers.

901 represents "p" or "b" sound plus a "z" or "s" sound, plus a "t" or "d" sound. It can be represented by the word ***bust***, ***past****e*, ***post*** and so on. Or use two words such as we***b suit*** or ***pass it***. Note that double

letters are pronounced as though there were only one – so they represent only ***one*** number. ***B**a**tt**e**r***, for example, would represent 914 ***not*** 9114.

5186 represents the sounds "L", "t" or "d", "f" or "v", and "sh", "j", "ch" or soft "g" – It could be represented by ***l**ea**d** **f**i**sh***, ***l**i**d** o**f*** a***sh***, ***l**igh**t** **f**i**sh***. Note in the last example that the "g" in "light" is not pronounced and therefore is ignored.

Now practice on your own. Make up words from the following numbers:

12
85
120
4684
57432

There are words and combinations of words you could have used including "ton," "file," "dance," "rush far," and "like Roman." Don't waste time trying to work them all into one word. Form two or three words; you can always link them together.

For example, if you want to remember the telelphone number 921-2975 you might come up with the words "pin it on back wall," or "paint knob cool" or "be not in bagel." Then to associate the words with a person, simply visualize that person pinning something on his back wall or painting the door knob a cool color, or climbing inside a giant bagel. It's easy to remember a phrase. But it's sometimes difficult to remember a number. Especially if you don't use it very often.

Practice converting telephone numbers to phrases or groups of words and see how easy it is to remember them. Then I'll show you some other practical applications of this number alphabet.

The uses of the number code are unlimited. But here are a few specific instances where I have found it useful. Before I start though, let me state that the best method of remembering numbers, like anything else, is to write them down. Then you only have to refer to them. So if you're in a restaurant or someone's office, don't attempt to commit the number to memory when you can simply jot it down in your telephone directory. There are many instances where this is impossible or impractical – and ***that's*** the time you use this memory gimmick.

If I'm driving to the airport, and I have to note the mileage reading in order to charge it back on my expenses, I simply convert the last three digits of the odometer reading to an object. I then associate that object in some way with the dashboard. Not only do I remember the number, more importantly ***I remember to remember the number***. (I used to forget to look at the odometer reading at the end of the trip.) For example, if the numbers were 410, I would convert it to "rats" and then I would picture a swarm of huge, vicious rats tearing apart the odometer on my dashboard. During the trip, whenever I glanced at my dashboard, I could visualize those rats. It would reinforce the image even more. At the end of the trip, a glance at my dashboard would once again bring the image to mind. I couldn't forget it if I ***wanted*** to. And "rats" can only be deciphered as 410. If I were to make another trip the same day, I would follow the same procedure. There's no fear of having more than one image re-enacting their scenes on the dashboard; the most recent image is the one that comes to mind first.

In working with numbers the same principles discussed in previous chapters apply. Make your images ridiculous, exaggerated, colorful, full of detail, with lots of action. The more vivid the better.

Now when I have arrived at the airport and parked, I make a point to look back at the car to visualize its position in relationship to its surroundings. Always do that. Especially in large plaza parking lots. But at the Toronto International Airport this doesn't help me very much since it's a continuous mass of concrete with not many identifiable landmarks. So I look at the parking spot number and as I rush to catch my plane, I make up a word and associate it with the car itself.

That particular lot has numbers A1, A2, B1, B2, etc. No problem. If the number were B4, I would convert the 4 to an "r," form the word "beer" and picture my car being swamped by a tidal wave of foaming beer. Or have hundreds of cans of beer falling out of the car as I open the door. When arriving back in Toronto two or more days later, I have never had trouble recalling the image and quickly translating it into the number – or in this case, combination of letter and number.

I find the number system helpful at conventions as well. It's so easy to memorize room numbers, including hospitality suites, and it saves a lot of time and inconvenience.

Even if I write the numbers down, I usually memorize the ones I know I will be needing. It's a terrible nuisance keeping track of the scraps of paper or programmes in my jacket, pants pocket or briefcase. In the case of room numbers, I always convert the number to an object and associate it in some way with the person (similar to the method described for telephone numbers in the previous chapter). So if Jack is in room 814, I might visualize Jack dressed like a "fighter," complete with purple shorts and boxing gloves. A reminder here that the "g" in fighter is silent. And if it's not pronounced, it's not used. There's usually a wide variety of words to choose from. In this case you could pick "Vader" (Darth Vader), "Fatter" (don't forget, double letters are pronounced as one), Fodder, Feeder, or a dozen others – each one translating into the number 814.

It's those short numbers like the combination on my lock at the club, a street address, the price of a product, a part number, that I used to have trouble with. Now I can quickly translate the number into an object, paint a mental picture – and presto! No more fear of forgetting. For example, I remembered that the number of that little white house on Turner Avenue in Chapter 12 was 49 because I pictured it being wrapped in "rope." The one on Page was covered with "mail."

And it works just as well for longer numbers. I've committed my driver's licence, social insurance number, OHIP number and some of my credit card numbers to memory. I have found it convenient to be able to recall them without having to dig them out of my wallet. Memorizing the hospital insurance number has been a real blessing since I normally don't have my cards with me at the times my children pick to break bones or otherwise mutilate themselves.

It's fun memorizing the longer numbers, because you can usually link the words together to form a story – which seems to stick forever in your memory.

And speaking of fun, there are many games you can play based on this system. I'll illustrate some in Chapter 19. But first, a few more practical uses.

Chapter 14

Statistics And Hockey Teams

Number Packages

If you want to remember statistics you can convert the numbers to words and lock the words together to form a story. Ignore the decimal point. Your common sense and natural memory will tell you where to put the decimal point when you convert from the word back to the number.

For example, assume you want to remember gross profit figures for the last ten years. Convert the numbers to words or groups of words as follows:

Year	*Gross Profit %*	*Code word(s)*
1972	11.5	Title
1973	20.2	Nose in
1974	28.0	Knives
1975	35.1	Mallet
1976	41.2	Rotten
1977	48.4	Roof air
1978	47.0	Rags
1979	49.8	Rip off
1980	51.1	Loaded
1981	53.9	Lamp

Now build a story in your mind by linking the words together. For example you may visualize a book with a *Title* standing out in large bold red letters.

You stick your ***nose in*** and it gets cut by ***knives*** buried in the pages. (Feel the pain, and the blood running from your nose; you won't forget it.)

You get mad and pound the book with a ***mallet***.

A ***rotten*** gas is emitted so you run to the roof for air. (Or hear yourself yelling "I'm going to get some ***roof air***." If you can visualize the scene, you won't forget the key words "roof" and "air.")

When you get to the roof, ***rags*** start falling from the sky.

They cover you and you quickly ***rip off*** these rags.

Then they are ***loaded*** into a truck.

The truck takes off but crashes into a ***lamp***.

With practice I guarantee you will have little difficulty making up these stories. And since you have to concentrate on the key words as you form them from the numbers, they settle in your long-term memory. The story allows you to recall them.

Put ***yourself*** into the story if you can. That way you can feel, smell, hear and see what is taking place. And don't forget to add lots of action.

If you have to know ***instantly*** the figure for 1978 or 1981, you could also apply the memory pegs described in Chapter 6. But for short lists such as this, I find it easy to quickly run through the story and stop at the figure I want.

There's no end to the applications for this system. I use it each year to quickly memorize the names and sweater numbers of my son's hockey team. It's so much more fun to know who number 21 is when he makes that dazzling move. Or number 77 when he scores with that blistering slap shot. You can use it for football teams, basketball teams, baseball teams, soccer teams – any kind of sport as long as they are identified by numbers. Here's last season's peewee hockey team for Goulding Park Rangers.

Sweater Number	*Key Word*	*Name*
2	Hcn	Joe
4	Ear	Craig
6	Ash	Tim
7	Ache	Scott
9	Ape	Chris
10	Dice	Sandford
15	Doll	Craig
16	Dish	Andrew
21	Nut	Robbie
22	Nun	Mike
27	Nag	Cary
29	Nap	Jeff
35	Mail	Shane
44	Rear	Jim
77	Kick	Sandro
99	Pop	Bryan

Now if you know what the boys look like, you can associate their faces directly with the key words, similar to the method used for names and faces in Chapter 10. For example, when you spot number 2 you will visualize Joe riding a ***hen*** around the arena. But early in the season, you don't even know what the individual players look like. In this case you would associate the name or a sound-alike with the corresponding number. Eventually of course, you will get to know the boys ***and*** their numbers without the necessity of keys.

Here's how I remembered the team.

2. Joe was the tallest boy on the team and easily identifiable. Otherwise I'd have pictured a "GI Joe" doll riding a hen. When I spotted "2" I'd think of "hen." I'd see a "GI Joe" riding that hen which would tell me it was "Joe."

4. Craig was my son. Not much difficulty here. But the name "Craig" could be represented by "Cragg" or "Egg." How about a giant "egg" with ears. When you spot number 4, you think of the key word "ear" – and you see the ridiculous image of ears on an egg. Egg reminds you of Craig.

6. I used "Tiny Tim" from the story about Scrooge. When I saw "6," the key word "ash" would come to mind. Then I would see "Tiny Tim" being buried in ashes – and I'd know it was Tim.

Get the idea? Try it on your local home team when the games are televised. It's easy.

Very quickly, here's the balance of my associations. Scott was represented by "Scott's Emulsion," a cod liver oil product I used to have to take as a child. Chris was a "cross." Sandford was a "Sand-filled Ford car" (close enough). Andrew was an "ant." Robbie was a "robber." Mike was a "microphone." Cary was something being "carried." Jeff was a "chef." Shane was a western hero, "Shane" (from a movie). Jim was "jam," Sandro was piles of "sand in a row." Bryan was a "briar patch."

If I spot number 21, which was "nut," I'd picture a "nut" being stolen by a "robber" – which would remind me of "Robbie." 29 translated as "nap" – and I'd see a "Chef" taking a nap. "Chef" told me the name was "Jeff."

When you make up your own associations be sure to make them unusual. For instance, that "chef" I mentioned was taking a "nap" on the middle of a table at a banquet, with his feet in somebody's plate. The more ridiculous the image, the faster it can be recalled. And it only takes seconds to paint elaborate pictures in your mind.

Chapter 15

Dates, Plates, Prices, And Postal Codes

Special Dates

To remember birthdays, anniversaries and other important dates, use the number code. Translate each month into its corresponding number. January is 1, February is 2, March is 3, etc. then make up 12 words, starting with "M" for month, and containing the sound which represents the number of the month. For example:

January (1) = Mud
February (2) = Mine
March (3) = Mum
April (4) = Mare
May (5) = Mail
June (6) = Match
July (7) = Mac
August (8) = Move
September (9) = Map
October (10) = Midas
November (11) = Matted
December (12) = Mitten

Now if your Aunt Sally's birthday is May 5th, quickly visualize a word that translates into 5, such as ***ale*** and see Aunt Sally putting a bottle of ***ale*** in the ***mail*** box. Jazz it up a little. See her putting a ribbon around the bottle, sticking a stamp on it, and squeezing it through the mail slot in a corner mailbox. Dwell on the scene for a minute or two to get it securely into your memory bank. Now, when you want to know Aunt Sally's birthday you will see Aunt Sally mailing a bottle of ale and it will remind you of the date: 5th month, 5th day – May 5th.

Practice. List all your relative's birthdays and convert them to word pictures. Here are a few of mine:

March 14 (My wife's birthday)	= Mom and tire I see my ***Mom*** presenting my wife with a huge ***tire*** complete with icing and candles
April 18 (My son's birthday)	= Mare and taffy I see my son opening a birthday gift and out jumps a white ***mare*** all stuck with ***taffy***
December 21 (My dad's birthday)	= Mitten and knit I see my Dad knitting a mitten. It's a huge, multicolored mitten.

Now, you wouldn't have to use this technique on your own family's birthdays. Nor do I. Except to use it as an example. But I ***do*** have trouble remembering all the anniversaries and birthdays of my friends and relatives. If you have the same trouble, use the above system. Apply it conscientiously and it won't fail you.

Licence Plates

If you have to remember car licence plates, which are a mixture of letters and numbers, simply make one word out of the letters and one out of the numbers. For example if a plate number is ADM 412, convert it to ***AD***A***M*** ROTTEN and associate these words with the car owner. Your natural memory will pick the right letters out of ***AD***A***M***. Try it. Here are some examples:

TRK 510 = ***TR***UC***K*** LOADS
VRY 101 = ***V***E***RY*** DUSTY
SDR 159 = ***S***A***D***DE***R*** TULIP

They don't always work out this easily. But no problem. Use two words where you have to. You will still be able to visualize them in some association with the car owner. For example:

BNR 151 = ***B***E***N***EA***R*** TOILET
XRY 298 = ***X***-***R***A***Y*** NO BEEF
GRT 162 = ***GR***EA***T*** TO CHIN

You can get plenty of practice while driving along the highway. See how quickly you can convert the licence plate numbers to meaningful words that you can visualize.

What's the practical use for memorizing licence plate numbers? Well, I've found it extremely useful. When a friend says "Just follow me. I know the way" I memorize his plate number as we start out. It's easy spotting the right car again once I lose him – which I invariably do. I've also found it useful when driving a rented car. Motels and service stations always seem to ask your licence plate number. And it's easy spotting a rented or borrowed car in a parking lot. It's also useful when passing the scene of an accident – or when you're involved in one yourself. The ability to be able to instantly memorize a licence plate until you have a chance to write it down could someday save someone's life or bring a criminal to justice.

Airline Flights

You can remember flight numbers the same way. It eliminates the inconvenience of having to repeatedly dig out your ticket to check your flight number. If it's a pure number, such as flight 187, simply convert it to meaningful words such as "tough guy." Associate it. See a tough looking guy boarding a plane. If there's a letter as part of the number such as F86, handle it as you would a licence plate. Make one word such as "fivish" or two words such as "half a fish" (the "l" in half is silent and is therefore meaningless). Your natural memory will tell you the first letter is an actual letter, and not to be translated into a number. Your gate number for departure can easily be remembered this way as well. Try it while waiting in line at customs or having a coffee. You'll find it's easy, fun, and great practice for those longer numbers such as telephone numbers.

Prices

If you have to compare prices and don't have a pencil or paper, use the number code system. I've found it quite handy when a friend tells me the price of something while I'm driving or at a party. If it's $19.27 use two words; one for 19 dollars and one for 27 cents. But it's not necessary. For here again, your natural memory will tell you it's $19.27 and not $1,927. – as well as your common sense. In this case you could pick "tap, nag" or "tap, knock" or "top, nick." Associate the words you select with the item. If a desk top calculator is $19.27, visualize the ***top*** with a ***nick*** out of it. The only way you could go wrong is to mix up the 19 and the 27 and come up with $27.19. Although your natural memory will probably tell you which one it is, it's safer to make sure you associate the first set of numbers directly to the object. For example, see the calculator, then the top, ***then*** the fact that there's a nick out of it. ***Consciously*** put the words in order and you will ***recall*** them in order.

Postal Codes

American zip codes are no problem – you simply convert the number to some meaningful phrase as we did for telephone numbers in Chapter 14.

Canadian postal codes are combinations of letters and numbers so they will have to treated more like licence plates. With one difference. Postal codes alternate letters with numbers. Thus we have M5A 1J8 or A1B 3S2. Nothing has to be left to actual memory since we can convert the code to 3 words beginning with the natural letter and ending with the "converted" sound. For example M5A 1J8 can be translated to MOLE ATE JEFF. When converting back to the original code, simply jot down the first letter of each word, combined with the number represented by the ending sound. MOLE ATE JEFF can only be M5A 1J8. Here a few more examples.

A1B 3S2 = AID BALMY SUN
L4T 9Z9 = LOWER TOP ZIP
B4B 1G7 = BEAR BIT GAG
B1P 5J4 = BAD PILL JAR
M1V 1L3 = MIGHTY FAT LAMB
N3T 5M8 = NAME TALL MOVIE

If you have trouble forming a phrase that makes sense, simply link three words together. For example, J4B 6H5 can be represented by JAR – BADGE – HILL and H9R 4R6 becomes HOP – REAR – RASH. Make up a short story so it sticks easier. See a ***jar*** wearing a ***badge*** and climbing a ***hill***. See the person ***hop*** in pain because his ***rear*** has a ***rash*** on it.

Since each of the three words only represent one letter followed by one number, you can use longer words, ignoring the superfluous numbers. For example, E2L 4L1 can be represented END LIARS LOT and converted back to E2L 4L1. The extra "D" and "S" would be ignored since you only use the first two consonant sounds. Another example would be C1A 7L1, represented by CAT AGGRAVATES LAD. All but the "A" and "G" in "aggravates" would be ignored.

Whether you end up with a catchy phrase, a series of linked words, or a brief picture story, don't forget to associate it in some way with the owner of the postal code.

Chapter 16

How To Memorize Scripture

Bible Study

The same techniques described earlier can be used to memorize scripture. As a start, the memory gimmicks described in Chapter 5 can be used to recall the number of books in the old and new testament. Count the number of letters as follows:

Old	Testament
3	9
New	Testament

Now, put 3 and 9 together, and you get 39 – the number of books in the old testament. ***Multiply*** 3 × 9 and you get 27 – the number of books in the new testament.

The story-telling system introduced in Chapter 5 can be used as well. Suppose you want to remember the 12 disciples.

Simon
James
John
Philip
Andrew
Bartholemew
Matthew
Thomas
James, son of Alphaeus
Thaddaeus
Simon, the Canaanite
Judas Iscariot

Simply make up a story in your mind, using the names of their sound alikes. Here's the story I made up to memorize them.

Simon the pieman, jammed ***(James)*** his pie in the john ***(John)*** filled it up ***(Philip)*** with water and drew ***(Andrew)*** it out. He placed it on the bar ***(Bartholemew)*** and dried it off with a mat ***(Matthew).*** A tom cat ***(Thomas)*** stole the pie and jammed it in Alf's pocket ***(James, son of Alphaeus).*** He was so sad ***(Thaddaeus)*** that Simon took a cane ***(Simon, the Canaanite)*** and hit him repeatedly until a Jew in a chariot ***(Judas Iscariot)*** rode up and grabbed the cane from him.

You don't have to use ***my*** story. Make up your own and actually visualize it taking place in your mind. Be sure to add action, color and make it as ridiculous as you like. The sillier it is, the easier you'll remember it.

Although I personally find it very easy to remember a story made up with the names or words I'm trying to remember, you might

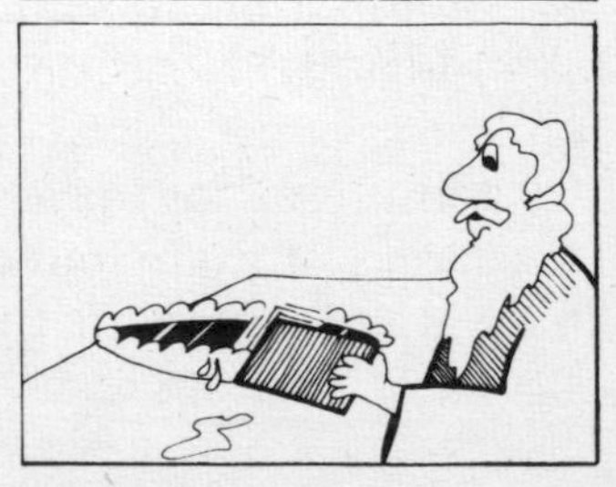

just want to associate pairs of words. Most memory books use this technique. In this case one name reminds you of the second name, the second name makes you recall the third name, and so on. Thus in the above example you might link Simon and James by visualizing Simon the pieman pouring tons of jam (James) into a gigantic pie shell. Be sure to exaggerate. The picture will have to stand out in your mind. See that jam overflowing the pie shell and covering Simon's boots – and the entire floor. Then link jam (James) with a john (John). Perhaps see someone shoveling jam into a john. Or if you pick a backhouse to represent a john, see someone opening the door and tons of jam flowing out.

I find that if you use the straight link system, without making it into a story, then visual images have to be more striking, unusual and exaggerated. But use whatever is easier for you.

There's no limit to what you can remember using this method. Suppose you have trouble remembering the twenty-seven books of the new testament in their proper order. Simply make up a story. Here's an example.

Matthew:	A little boy called ***Matthew***
Mark:	***Marked*** (Mark)
Luke:	A bag of ***loot*** (Luke)
John:	and threw it in the ***john*** (John)
Acts:	Then he started ***acting*** (Acts) up
Romans:	Some ***Roman*** soldiers (Romans) came and shook him. They took two apples from him, ate them, and threw the ***first core***
First Corinthians:	(First Corinthians) into the john,
Second Corinthians:	and then threw the ***second core*** (Second Corinthians) into the john
Galatians:	The cores joined together to form a huge ***glacier*** (Galatians)
Ephesians:	On top of the glacier someone was having a ***feast*** (Ephesians)

Philippians:	It was prince ***Philip*** (Philippians)
Colossians:	Philip wrote a ***colossal*** (Colossians) thesis
First Thessalonians:	The first ***thesis*** (First Thessalonians) he gave away and
Second Thessalonians:	The ***second thesis*** (Second Thessalonians) he gave away –
First Timothy:	The ***First, to Timothy*** (First Timothy)
Second Timothy:	and the ***second to Timothy*** as well (Second Timothy)
Titus:	Timothy rolled them ***tight*** (Titus)
Philemon:	and ***filled a man*** (Philemon) with them (visualize him jamming them into someone's mouth)
Hebrews:	The man was a ***Hebrew*** (Hebrew)
James:	and having them ***jammed*** (James) in his mouth made him feel ill
First Peter:	He ***first,*** started to ***peter*** out even more (First Peter)

Second Peter:	***Secondly,*** he started to ***peter*** out even more (Second Peter)
First John:	***First*** he went to the ***john,*** ill (First John)
Second John:	***Secondly,*** he went to the ***john*** again (Second John)
Third John:	***Thirdly,*** he went to the ***john*** yet again (Third John) This time he fell in
Jude:	And a ***Jew*** (Jude) saved him
Revelations:	***revealing*** himself (Revelations) to be a hero.

Any story you make up doesn't have to be realistic or sensible. That's the beauty of stories that are only in your mind. And the word-clues don't have to be that great. "Core" is enough to remind you of Corinthians and "thesis" is enough to remind you of Thessalonians.

Try it. Read the story to yourself a few times, actually visualizing the events in your minds eye. After a surprisingly short period of time, the images will flash into your mind, with their corresponding meanings, very quickly. And you'll never have trouble thumbing to a specific book in the bible again.

By using the number code you can also remember how many chapters there are in each book. Pick words to represent the numbers (as we did in

Chapter 13). Then link these words to the clue words representing the books of the New Testament as follows.

Book	*No. of Chapters*	*Code word for the number*
Matthew	28	enough
Mark	16	touch
Luke	24	near
John	21	naughty
Acts	28	knave
Romans	16	tish
1 Corinthians	16	dish
2 Corinthians	13	dam
Galatians	6	age
Ephesians	6	hash
Philippians	4	heir
Colossians	4	air
1 Thessalonians	5	will
2 Thessalonians	3	hymn
1 Timothy	6	wish
2 Timothy	4	row
Titus	3	ham
Philemon	1	odd
Hebrews	13	tam
James	5	all
1 Peter	5	ill
2 Peter	3	home
1 John	5	hole
2 John	1	hit
3 John	1	die
Jude	1	tie
Revelations	22	nun

Now you can link the code word which represents the number to the word that you previously picked to represent the chapter. Actually build it into your story.

So you would visualize the boy "Matthew" and his mother telling him that's ***enough*** (28). He "marks" the loot and she says, "Don't ***touch***" (16). The "loot" is ***near*** (24). When he throws it in the "john," she yells, "***naughty***" (21). He "acts" up and she calls him a ***knave*** (28). Meanwhile the "Romans" arrive and say, "***tish,*** tish" (16). They throw first one "core" in the ***dish*** (16) and then the second "core" forms a ***dam*** (13). The "glacier" is associated with and ice ***age*** (6). The "feast" consists of ***hash*** (6). "Prince Phillip" is the ***heir*** (4). And his "colossal" thesis is as big as ***air*** itself (4). The "First thesis" is a ***will*** (5). The "second thesis" is a ***hymn*** (3). When he gives the first one to Timothy, he ***wishes*** (6) for more. But when he gives the second one to Timothy he causes a ***row*** (4). He rolls it as "tight" as a ***ham*** (3). He "fills a man" with it – which is ***odd*** (1). The man turns out to be a "Hebrew" wearing a ***tam*** (13). It was "jammed" in his mouth – ***all*** (5) of it. He "first petered" out and became ***ill*** (5) and went ***home*** (3). He went to the "john" and fell in the ***hole*** (5). When he went to the "second john" he ***hit*** (1) the bottom. When he went to the "third john" he thought he'd ***die*** (1). But the "Jew" pulled him out with a ***tie*** (1). He "revealed" himself to be a hero and was cheered on by a ***nun*** (22).

It's easier to ***do*** than explain. Simply build your own story with the "clue" words as key words in the story. You may be able to commit to memory the names of the twenty-seven books of the new testament in the proper sequence, along with the number of chapters in each book, in less than twenty minutes. Or it may take you two hours. But once you have succeeded, you will have trouble ***forgetting them***.

You can memorize scripture the same way. For example, whenever I find myself worrying about something, I like to remind myself of Philippians 4:6-7

> "Do not be anxious about anything,
> but in everything by prayer and
> petition, with thanksgiving, present
> your requests to God. And the peace
> of God, which transcends all under-
> standing, will guard your hearts and
> your minds in Christ Jesus."
> – Philippians 4:6-7

Since the "clue" or "peg" word that I use for Philippians is "Prince Phillip," I see ***Prince Phillip*** very ***worried***. So much so that he is tearing out his ***hair*** (4) and tossing it among some ***ash(es)*** 6. This gives me the reference, Philippians 4:6. (My "natural" memory tells me verse 7 is also included, but you can throw in another picture, like ***egg*** if you want.)

Then comes the verse itself. I visualize someone telling Prince Phillip not be ***anxious*** about anything. Then I see him kneeling down and ***praying***. He holds up a ***petition*** and a turkey (***thanksgiving***) is tearing at that petition.

Here's how the mind works. If you have read over the verse several times, and you understand it, clues like these will bring the verse to mind almost word for word.

Once you see an anxious or worried Phillip, you will ***know*** the verse starts "Do not be anxious about anything." And when you see him ***praying***, and holding up a ***petition***, you will know it continues "But in everything by prayer and petition." The turkey will force you to recall "with thanksgiving."

Continue to paint your picture story. Visualize a ***present*** being presented to a ***King*** (representing God), and a ***piece*** of that ***King*** rising (***transcending***) past a book of knowledge (***understanding***). See it opening a jail and tossing in some ***hearts*** and ***minds*** and blocking the door with a giant cross (representing ***Christ Jesus***).

Now see how easy it is to recall the actual verse as you unravel the links that make up your word picture. "***Present*** your requests to God. And the ***peace of God*** which ***transcends*** all ***understanding*** will guard your ***hearts*** and your ***minds*** in ***Christ Jesus***."

Chapter 17

Fun And Games

Memory Magic

Once you've practiced the techniques described in this book you can enjoy yourself by posing as a memory expert or mind reader.

My favourite "game" is to assign a different number to everyone at a party and then recall that number instantly upon request – even a year later. Or longer. As long as you remember the person's name, you will remember the number. Because the number is simply the name transposed into a number.

For example, if the person's name were Paul Campbell, his number would be 957395. So you simply make the rounds, writing the corresponding numbers on slips of paper and handing them to the corresponding individuals. When you get to Pat Thornton, you say "Okay Pat, I think I'll assign you 9114212!" You say the digits out loud as you slowly translate the name in your mind, writing them down as you do so. Here are some sample names with their corresponding numbers:

Bill Fraser	958404
Keith Chamberlain	71639452
Milt Pogson	3519702
David Bloom	181953
Raymond Quirk	4321647
Rod Harding	414127

Usually everyone will be amazed as you make the rounds again, relating "from memory" the numbers you assigned them. The fact that you relate the number ***slowly***, one digit at a time, as you sound out the name to yourself, merely gives the impression of deep concentration. As though you are actually digging the numbers out of your memory.

If you want to make it look ***really*** difficult, add a sentence to the name. For example, say to yourself, "Albert Baker is a stupid moron." You shouldn't forget that! And it would translate into 594197400191342 – an almost impossible number to memorize so quickly.

If you want to set someone up as a "mind reader," tip off a friend in advance that you will be calling throughout the evening with coded messages. And explain the code. Tell the people at the party that you know of someone who can read minds. All they have to do is write any two digit number on a piece of paper, concentrate on it, and your friend can tell them the number – by phone!

Let's assume someone thinks of the number 24. Translate it in your mind to something that will be easy to include in a sentence. "Near" is good enough. Phone your friend. Explain that you will be letting someone talk to him and that this person will be concentrating on a two digit number. End your conversation with the word "near." For example, "Okay Bob, let's see if you can be dead on. It's no good just being near." Your partner in deceit knows in advance that the last word you say translates into the number. And therefore the number can only be "24." If he's a real ham he can really drag it out with such dramatics as "concentrate on the number. I see a two. The other digit is not very clear. Please trace over it with your finger. Try to re-write it in your mind. Wait. Now I've got it. It's a 4. The number is 24."

I picked two-digit numbers since it's much easier and faster to translate them into words and back again. But you can be really adventurous if you like and use three, four or more digits, translating them into longer words or a series of two or more words which you feed to your partner in some prearranged code.

It's easy to make up a sentence ending with the code word. Here are some examples:

71	"Make it ***good.***"
25	"Hit it on the ***nail.***"
36	"Your skill can't be ***matched.***"
98	"Show her you're not a ***buff.***"
42	"Hope you'll be right as ***rain.***"

Note that your mind-reading friend will know it's only a two digit number, and in the case of ***matched*** will take the first two digits only, 3 and 6, and ignore the last one.

The above feats can be performed with a very basic knowledge of the techniques used in this book. If you become ***skilled*** with the techniques, you can perform all kinds of astounding demonstrations including card tricks, memorizing the pages of magazines, or quickly memorizing one hundred numbers.

But if you did that, you ***would*** be a memory expert. And that's not the purpose of this book. But don't let me discourage you from trying more complicated feats. If you're really interested, get a copy of some of the reference books I've listed. They all contain good ideas – or at least a reinforcement of what you already know.

Chapter 18

A Week In The Life Of...

Taylor Takes A Trip

If you use these techniques all the time, they become a habit. A very useful habit. For example, let me review the various ways I put these memory devices to use this past week. I must admit it was an unusual week, inasmuch as I had to rush my wife to the hospital in an ambulance on Monday night. A false alarm, but a scary one. And an experience that made me thankful for my memory techniques. We can forget telephone numbers under times of stress. But I found I didn't forget the visual image of my wife's brother-in-law nailing a "juicy spare rib" to his front door and his wife yelling, ***"No nail juicy rib."*** (Which translated, as I dialed, to 225-6049.) We had to make the call to insure someone would look after a three-year-old while we made the trip. And at the emergency ward of Scarborough General Hospital, I had to give the secret password – my hospital insurance number – before being allowed to see my wife. I had no trouble seeing that china dish on the operating table being administered a transfusion while the nurse muttered ***"dish lives two days."*** 16580110. If you cannot imagine ever being without your insurance card or list of telephone numbers, try to imagine how organized you'd be if your spouse had a heart attack in the middle of the night. It takes very little time to memorize some emergency telephone numbers. So make sure that those of your doctor, ambulance, police, fire department, and hospital are among them.

On Tuesday I had to fly to Sydney, Nova Scotia (via Halifax) to conduct a memory training seminar. I drove to the airport, and as I left my house, I glanced at the odometer on the dash-board, converting the last three digits, 775 to ***"cackle."*** I imagined a hen cackling on my dash-board as he pecked away at the odometer. When I arrived at the Toronto International Airport, I again checked the reading. It was now 805. I could have converted it to ***"vessel,"*** but it was the ***elapsed mileage*** that I had to remember for my expense account, so I subtracted and converted the resulting 30 kms. to ***"mice."*** I visualized a violent scene of hundreds of mice attacking that hen on my dash-board – just in case it was a while before I was able to jot that figure down. When I parked in space "5L" I glanced back at my car and visualized a huge ***"lily"*** growing out of the roof. (Since all the spaces in the lot were a combination of a letter and a number, there was no fear of mistakingly translating it back to "55".)

As it happened, I had no opportunity to record those figures since I had a briefcase in one hand, a suitcase in the other, and no time to stop along the way.

On arriving in the terminal building I checked my flight on the T.V. monitor to make sure the plane was leaving on time, and to check the gate number. I had already converted (two days earlier) my flight number and departure time. It was flight "624" leaving at 12:45 p.m. – which to me, was ***"joiner"*** at the ***"tin rail."*** I had painted a mental picture of joining my wife at a bar called the Tin Rail. I saw that the departure gate was number 76, so I added "cash" to my image. Now I was to ***"joiner"*** at the ***"Tin Rail"*** with ***"cash."***

I had plenty of time to reinforce the images as I lined up to have my bag checked and to make my seat selection.

If all this seems unnecessary, it probably is for someone who never forgets an odometer reading or doesn't mind pulling their plane ticket out of their pocket to keep checking flight number, departure time, or gate number. ***But the practice is invaluable.*** The more you use the system, the more proficient you become. Once inside the plane, I jotted down the mileage reading and parking lot number. The purpose of these memory systems is not to hold facts in your mind forever – simply for the length of time you ***need*** them.

While on the plane I also memorized my connections at Halifax. I was scheduled to leave on flight 102 at 7:40 p.m. I converted this to ***"toes in egg rice"*** and I pictured myself with my toes stuck in a plate of egg rice. Later, I found out my departure gate was "14" which became ***"tire"*** – something I pictured myself munching on. The fact that I still remember these numbers a week later proves how effective the system is. But don't worry about cluttering your mind with useless flight numbers or parking-lot numbers. They'll fade in time. In fact, they usually fade very quickly. Only those important numbers that you ***want*** to remember will remain forever.

On Wednesday, I conducted the all-day training programme for the National Secretaries Association of Cape Breton. No need to mention the importance of a memory system for names, facts and figures in this type of situation.

One new use of the system was introduced, however, showing its extreme adaptability.

Together, the group memorized the various positions and people comprising the 1981 seminar committee. Here is what they memorized in about fifteen minutes:

Chairman	– Pat Rideout
Hotel & Hospitality Arrangements	– Selma Rudderham
Exhibitors	– Audrey Gouthro
Door Prizes	– Vicki Devereaux
Information Kits	– Ellen Aucoin
Registration	– Darla Brown
	– Ellen MacLean
Publicity	– Donna Wall
Membership	– Carol Gill
CPS & Education	– Judy Turner
Audit	– Sharon Roper

We built a story, starting with the ***Chairman*** who ***patted*** (Pat) a horse and started to ***ride out*** (Rideout) of the ***hotel.*** The word "hotel" was enough of a clue to tell us the next position, "Hotel and Hospitality Arrangements." When she got out of the hotel she tried to ***Sell Ma*** (Selma) a rudder (Rudderham). It didn't sell so she put it on ***exhibit*** (Exhibitors). Something ***odd*** (Audrey) happened. She wanted to ***go throw*** it (Gouthro) at a ***door*** (Door Prizes). When it hit, the door became ***icky and sticky*** (Vicki) and she had to ***dive through*** it (Devereaux) into a pile of ***Information Kits.*** When she hit the kits, ***coins*** (Aucoin) fell out – hundreds of them with "***Ls***" on them (Ellen). She used the coins to pay her ***registration*** fee (Registration) and was waited on by a ***darling brown*** girl (Darla Brown) who gave her a ***MacLean's*** Magazine (MacLean) containing an article on ***Hell*** (Ellen). It was full of advertising and ***publicity*** (Publicity) including a beautiful girl ***donning*** (Donna) a dazzling evening gown and sitting on a ***wall*** (Wall). She used the wall to keep the ***members*** (Membership) from getting into the seminar. But they jumped on the wall and started singing ***carols*** (Carol) with their ***gills*** (Gill).

This was a real ***education*** (CPS & Education) for her and she ***turned*** (Turner) to a ***Jew*** (Judy) and asked for an ***audit*** (Audit). The audit revealed that all the association owned was ***rope*** (Roper) which was ***shared*** (Sharon) among the membership.

The fact that the "story" was far-fetched did not make it more difficult to recall. One quick review, and the participants were able to rhyme off the positions and the people who held those positions.

Thursday morning was spent flying back to Toronto and I used the same techniques for flight numbers, times and departure gates for the return trip. I had no trouble recalling my parking spot at Toronto International Airport. I just thought of the car, saw the huge ***lily*** sticking out of the roof, and translated it to 5L. On the way to the office I made a mental "things to do" list using the memory key 1 – wand, 2 – swan, etc. I was up to eight items when I arrived at the office, and I quickly jotted them down on my daily planning calendar. (Don't press your luck by keeping things in your memory when you have an opportunity to write them down.)

On Friday, I took the afternoon off work because it was my youngest son's birthday. We booked into a hotel and spent the afternoon swimming, playing pinball, table tennis. I really didn't have anything to memorize except the room number. That came in handy, since I left the room without the key (on purpose, mind you) to visit the gift shop. Number 701 converted easily to "***cost***" and was very appropriate since I had to pay $40 just to use the room for the afternoon.

On Saturday evening we were invited out to dinner. Bob Cronish phoned and gave me directions on how to get to his house. I scribbled them down as he talked. "Go along 401 to Spadina

Expressway. Go south to Eglinton. East on Eglinton to Bathurst. South on Bathurst, 3 lights to Burton. Turn east on Burton to first lights and turn right (south) on Glen Ayr. Our house is number 584, the fifth house on the left-hand side."

I visualized myself driving as he talked and felt myself turning left every time he said to turn east. Then, when he hung up, I quickly memorized the directions by painting the following story in my mind: Bob took a ***spade*** (Spadina) and smashed an ***egg*** (Eglinton) with it. It splattered all over him, so he took a ***bath*** (Bathurst). But there in the bath tub was ***Richard Burton*** (Burton) holding ***three flashlights*** (to tell me I go three lights before turning). Bob grabbed the ***first light*** (to tell me I go one light before turning) and made it vanish into ***thin air*** (Glen Ayr). I visualized a "***lover***" (584) on the front lawn. Since I was familiar with the real street names, only a slight clue was needed to bring them to mind. And since I only had to turn either east or south to get to Bob's place, I had no fear of turning the wrong way.

Sunday was relaxation day. The only thing I consciously memorized was a verse from the new testament. I try to memorize at least one new verse each week. Scripture isn't really that difficult because it has its own story form without the necessity of creating one. But you have to understand it. And because of the unusual phrases and expressions, I find it easier, initially, to use sound-alikes and symbols to get the phrases into my long-term storage system.

On Sunday I memorized Philippians 4:19. "And my God will meet all your needs according to His glorious riches in Christ Jesus." I converted 4:19 to "hair top" and pictured Prince Philip's hair top (toupé) being lifted by a king (God). The king meets a bunch of animated knees (meets all your needs). The knees have accordians strapped to them (according). The accordians split open spilling out jewels and diamonds which are scooped up by my sister-in-law, Gloria (glorious riches) and stuffed inside a cross (Christ Jesus). I find that every word doesn't have to be converted to a sound-alike – only enough to clue in my natural memory. And although visualizing a ridiculous scene such as the one above allows me to recall the actual wording, eventually this memory aid is unnecessary. But I've also found that if I haven't recited it for awhile, and it has started to fade from my memory, visualizing those images allows me to fish it out of long-term storage.

I didn't hear any jokes worth remembering that week. Nor did I have occasion to memorize licence plates, postal codes, dates, speeches or prices. But rarely a week goes by without having to make use of most of the memory techniques described in this book.

CONCLUSION

Don't give up. The first time I was confronted with a book on memory, I was overwhelmed by all the techniques and examples. I thought, "There's no way I have time to absorb all this!"

But the hardest part of accomplishing anything is the ***thought*** of it. Once we dig in our heels and try something, it's never as difficult as it seemed at first glance. And the more we keep at something, the easier it becomes.

This book does not have a lot of different techniques. It simply consists of examples of how the same basic techniques can be applied to a variety of situations.

The key to an effective memory is motivation. How badly do you ***want*** to remember? Is it worth a half-hour a day? Twenty minutes a day? Well, in just twenty minutes a day, over the course of a few months, you can memorize those peg words and the number code backwards and forwards. As far as visualizing crazy scenes is concerned, you ***can*** do it. Some people have a mental block at first – but that's only because they ***think*** they can't. If you think you can't, you won't. But if you think you can, you will. Practice. If you still have problems, use the buddy system. Get a friend or a family member to practice the "mind games" with you. It'll be fun. In fact hilarious. It's amazing how ridiculous (and unforgettable) the associations can become when two or more people are involved.

Names and faces give most people trouble. Try the association technique everytime you meet someone for the first time. Don't be discouraged if you don't succeed right away. Failure is just another word for quitting. Keep trying. The associations will come easier and faster the longer you work at it. Even if you ***can't*** link the name to the face with some ridiculous association, the effort itself will force you to truly observe the person's face. And you will be forced to really ***hear*** the person's name – or ask to have it repeated. And by paying attention, showing interest, repeating the name aloud and to yourself, you'll discover that recalling the name later isn't really as difficult as it used to be.

Make listening and observing a habit. You'll not only get more out of your memory – you'll get more out of life. Review this book frequently. It has enough techniques and examples to launch you on the path to a better memory. Good luck.

And don't forget!

Bibliography

Best, Graham, ***Memory Made Easy,*** Beaverlodge, Alberta: Horizon Books (published by Horizon House Publishers) 1980.

Byrne, Brendan, ***Three Weeks To A Better Memory,*** New York: Bantam Books (by arrangement with John C. Winston Company), 1956.

Dineen, Jacqueline, ***Remembering Made Easy,*** Toronto, Canada: Coles Publishing Company Limited, 1979.

Furst, Dr. Bruno, ***Stop Forgetting,*** Garden City, New York: Doubleday & Company Inc., (Revised and expanded edition by Lotto Furst and Gerrit Storm), 1979.

Kellett, Michael C., ***How To Improve Your Memory And Concentration,*** New York: Monarch Press (a Simon & Schuster Division of Gulf & Western Corporation), 1977.

Laird, Donald A. and Eleanor C. Laird, ***Techniques for Efficient Remembering,*** New York: McGraw-Hill Book Company, Inc., 1960.

Logan, Col. Arthur L., ***Increase Your Memory,*** Toronto, Canada: Coles Publishing Company Limited, 1976.

Lorayne, Harry, ***Remembering People,*** New York: Stein and Day Publishers (first published in 1975), n.d.

Lorayne, Harry, ***How To Develop A Super-Power Memory,*** New York: Signet Books (The New American Library, Inc.), 1974.

Lorayne, Harry and Jerry Lucas, ***The Memory Book,*** New York: Ballantine Books (by arrangement with Stein and Day Publishers), 1975.

Lorayne, Harry, ***How To Pass Any Subject,*** Toronto Canada: Coles Publishing Company Limited, 1978.

Markoff, David and Denise Carcel, ***Total Recall,*** New York: Charter Books (A Division of Charter Communications, Inc.), 1979.

Montgomery, Robert L., ***Memory Made Easy,*** New York: AMACOM (A division of American Management Associations), 1979.

Young, Chesley V., ***The Magic of A Mighty Memory,*** New York: Parker Publishing Co., Inc., 1972.